A HOUSE
THAT
MADE
HISTORY

"To this place, and the kindness of these people, I owe every thing.
Here I have lived a quarter of a century, and have passed from a young to an old man.
Here my children have been born, and one is buried.
I now leave, not knowing when, or whether ever, I may return . . ."
—ABRAHAM LINCOLN

UPON HIS DEPARTURE FROM SPRINGFIELD, ILLINOIS, TO HIS
PRESIDENTIAL INAUGURATION IN WASHINGTON D.C., FEBRUARY 11, 1861

A HOUSE
THAT
MADE
HISTORY

The Illinois Governor's Mansion
Legacy of an Architectural Treasure

MK PRITZKER
First Lady of Illinois

Foreword by Michael S. Smith

RIZZOLI
NEW YORK

New York · Paris · London · Milan

PREVIOUS PAGES The Governor's Mansion today retains elements both of its original Italianate and Greek Revival features and of those added during a late-nineteenth-century remodeling.

The original elliptical staircase of the mansion was recreated as part of the 1970–1971 remodeling initiated by First Lady Dorothy Shriver Ogilvie. New floors of wood and reclaimed Spanish marble tile were added during the Pritzker administration.

LEFT Theodore Roosevelt (center), pictured here with Governor Richard Yates Jr. (far left), visited the Governor's Mansion as vice president in 1901 before touring Camp Lincoln. The group, including First Lady Helen Wadsworth Yates (seated next to her mother-in-law, the former First Lady Catharine Geers Yates), posed on the portico.

ABOVE A photographic portrait of Frederick Douglass made by George Kendall Warren captures the gravity and dignity of the renowned statesman, speaker, and author, who visited the mansion in 1872.

OPPOSITE The daughter of a wealthy Springfield real estate baron, First Lady Cora Edith English Tanner combined elegance with intellect and a commitment to human rights.

FOLLOWING PAGES The youthful Tanner Cadets standing in formation in front of the mansion in 1898 during the time of the Spanish-American War. The portico had been embellished with flags and bunting, including two Cuban flags that were hung in support. Posters of heroes Admiral Dewey, Admiral Sampson, Admiral Schley, and Major General Nelson Miles were displayed on the columns.

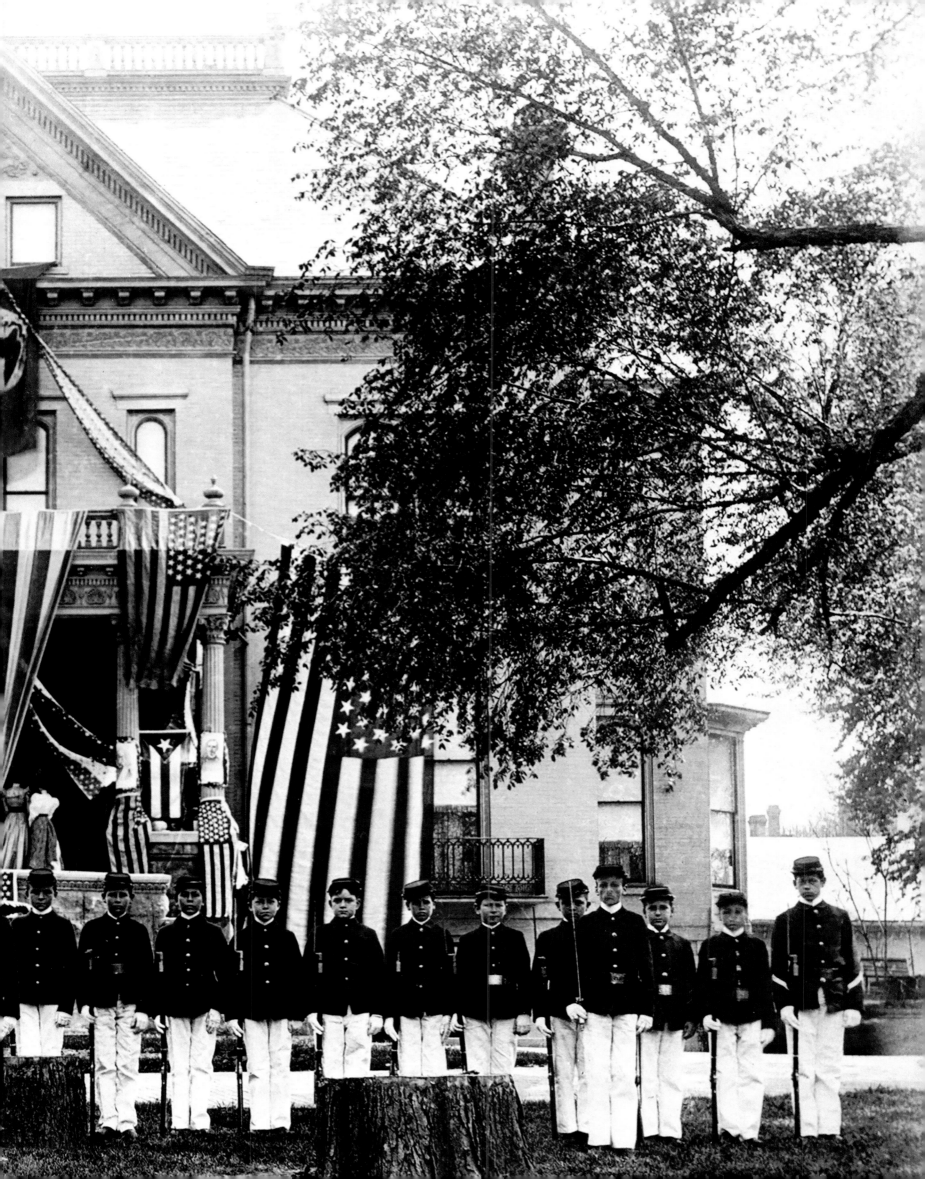

This book is dedicated to
the people of Illinois.

JB and I thank you for the trust
you have placed in us and the
opportunity to serve you.
Being your governor and first lady
has been the greatest
honor of our lives.

MK PRITZKER
FIRST LADY

JB PRITZKER
GOVERNOR

CONTENTS

FOREWORD

MICHAEL S. SMITH

I met MK and JB Pritzker the night before the 2009 Obama inauguration. We were introduced by our mutual friend Desirée Rogers, who was the White House social secretary for the incoming administration. From the very beginning, I could see that the Pritzkers were a dynamic and deeply engaging couple. MK and I became fast friends, and over the years, I worked on a few design projects for them. Nearly a decade later, when JB was elected governor of Illinois in 2018, MK asked me to collaborate with her on the decoration of the Governor's Mansion in Springfield. Not only was she very familiar with my interiors for President and Mrs. Obama at the White House, but we also shared a great respect for the architectural and design legacy of the Illinois mansion and an understanding that any changes we made should keep the needs of future governors and their families top of mind.

MK's passion for the project was clear from the outset, and I think she has done a brilliant job. With a vision of celebrating the beauty and fascinating history of the mansion and showcasing the extraordinary artistry and talent of the people of Illinois, she has transformed a stately, rather austere house into one that is at once formal and impressive and warmly welcoming. Challenged with updating public rooms that must accommodate a range of functions—from large receptions for state legislators and holiday parties to intimate gatherings and student tour groups—MK has imbued these historic spaces with a relaxed elegance, renewed energy, and clear sense of joy.

Our work started with a strong foundation, as the greatest asset of the mansion is a classic floor plan with a graceful flow. The house also features a remarkable collection of furnishings, art, and artifacts that we put to good use, employing a serene, sophisticated palette to mix disparate periods, styles, and provenance into a cohesive whole.

One of my favorite spaces is the Lincoln Parlor, which features magnificent Greek Revival architectural detail that was less evident previously when the room was painted white. We decided to cover the walls in a custom-made green moiré fabric that now enhances the distinctive millwork, in addition to making the spacious room feel more intimate and inviting. In the adjacent Music Parlor, we used a matching moiré in a sumptuous blue, and the East and West Parlors are clad in a sophisticated yellow-and-white stripe. Throughout the house, we employed subtle, colorful backgrounds that enliven the interiors and complement MK's selection of art, which ranges from historical portraits of President Lincoln on loan from the nearby Abraham Lincoln Presidential Library and Museum to contemporary works by leading Illinois artists.

As MK and I worked to refine the interiors of the Governor's Mansion, we were extremely conscious that as governor and first lady, JB and MK were stewards and protectors of an official residence and family home with a storied past and a future full of promise. This book documents its stunning historic rooms, which now reflect a burnished beauty and renewed relevance, in addition to the spirit and commitment of the Pritzkers themselves.

ABOVE A sculpture entitled *Growing Flowing* displayed in the Lincoln Parlor's bay window is the work of Richard Hunt. Born on Chicago's South Side in 1935, Hunt was the first Black American sculptor to be the subject of a solo exhibition at the Museum of Modern Art, New York, in 1971.

OPPOSITE Named the Kankakee Room, the second-floor sitting room features a portrait in the style of artist George Romney, whose career in the late eighteenth century coincided with the growing popularity of Zuber & Cie's wood-blocked panoramic wallpaper.

LEFT The East Garden features a cast-iron fountain that has been a fixture of the grounds since 1887. It was moved from its first location in the front of the mansion to the side garden during the Rauner administration in 2018.

INTRODUCTION

Growing up in South Dakota, I never imagined that I would become the first lady of Illinois and that the grand old house known as the People's House would become my home. It was by chance that in my junior year at the University of Nebraska I was offered an internship in the office of Senator Tom Daschle in Washington, D.C. Studying interior design and planning to pursue a post-graduate degree in preservation architecture, I wasn't sure I wanted to add politics to my education, but I was game for a summer adventure. As it turned out, I loved working in government and my internship grew into a staff assistant job and a semester off from school. Autumn of that year, I was set up on a blind date with JB Pritzker, who worked across the hall on the third floor of the Hart Senate Office Building, and, as they say, the rest is history.

The largest governor's residence in the country and one of the oldest and most beautiful, the Governor's Mansion in Springfield, Illinois, has a storied history intertwined with the lives of its residents, our great state, and our country. From within the hallowed halls of this house, our state has helped shape the nation, most often for the better. The stories this house tells are so fascinating that I felt compelled to share them. Illinois has had forty-three governors, many of whom have made important contributions to the state and the nation. I have chosen to relate the stories of the most influential and fascinating of these, as well as their most famous visitors and first ladies—women who made substantial improvements to state and national social welfare while also tending to the mansion. One of a first lady's responsibilities is to ensure that the mansion offers a suitable backdrop against which the business of state can take place outside the formal halls of the capitol. This is not simply the act of creating an attractive home—it is an aid to governance.

The mansion has been home to Illinois's governors since 1855, and as styles have shifted, so, too, has its interior design. Its architecture has changed as well, reflecting varied aesthetics and philosophies of preservation and renovation. Cultural and technological evolutions have also played a role in shaping the mansion's form and footprint. This multi-layered story is related in the following pages through contemporaneous descriptions, photographs, floor plans, and drawings left to us by architects, designers, and occupants, past and present. They bring to life the surroundings created by, lived in, and worked among by the state's highest officers and families since 1855. The most recent refurbishment, completed in 2021, is also documented in photographs for future historians, architects, and designers.

In the years just prior to his election to the presidency, Abraham Lincoln regularly walked the halls of the Governor's Mansion in friendship with William H. Bissell, the second governor to occupy it. A few years later, thrice-elected governor Richard J. Oglesby became one of the very last people to spend time with Lincoln on the day of his assassination in 1865. Illinois's own Ulysses S. Grant visited the mansion many times, and as president is believed to have penned his remarks honoring Lincoln at the 1874 dedication of his tomb at Oak Ridge Cemetery in one of its rooms. In 1893, Governor John P. Altgeld, whose courageous actions influenced the labor movement in this country forever, assumed residency in the mansion. In the mid-twentieth century, President

OPPOSITE An oil painting on panel by Craig Blietz is among the twentieth- and twenty-first-century artworks First Lady MK Pritzker has chosen to ornament the mansion's rooms in honor of the Illinois artists who created them.

FOLLOWING PAGES A line of women in gloves and hats in the 1950s waiting to attend a tea, hosted by First Lady Shirley Breckenridge Stratton for the Parent-Teacher Association, winds through the front lawn of the mansion. Mrs. Stratton also started a new tradition by opening the house for tours in 1960.

Harry S. Truman recruited Governor Adlai E. Stevenson II to run for the presidency. Stevenson, who wrote his concession speech in his mansion office, is said to have brought a new generation into politics, setting the stage for the election of the nation's youngest president, John F. Kennedy. Half a century later, mere blocks from the mansion on the steps of the Old State Capitol where Lincoln delivered his "House Divided" speech, a young Black junior United States senator from Illinois, Barack Obama, launched his bid for the presidency of the United States.

This book is the story of the People's House and the people of Illinois to whom it belongs. It is their spirit, strength, and resolve that has established the state's long tradition of leading the way for positive social change. They are the citizens who elected leaders who went on to make Illinois the first state to pass both the Thirteenth Amendment abolishing slavery and the Nineteenth Amendment granting women the full right to vote. Illinois's most famous daughter, Hillary Clinton, became a first lady, a United States senator, secretary of state, and the first woman ever to win the presidential nomination from a major party. This state has produced other groundbreaking women, including Nobel Peace Prize-winner Jane Addams, Jackie Joyner-Kersee, one of the greatest athletes of all time, U.S. senators Carol Moseley Braun and Tammy Duckworth, First Lady Michelle Obama, and civil rights leader Ida B. Wells. Illinois has also nurtured the curious and creative minds of Frank Lloyd Wright, Mies van der Rohe, Carl Sandburg, Sandra Cisneros, Gwendolyn Brooks, and John Prine.

The greatness of our state has its origins among the farmers who tilled the fertile soil that now feeds much of the world, the boat captains and stevedores who worked Lake Michigan and the rivers that now help deliver goods across the globe, and the innovators who introduced railroads, interstate highways, and airports. Long before our state came into being, it was the center of the largest pre-Columbian settlement north of Mexico and later home to the Sauk, Meskwaki, Potawatomi, Kickapoo, Ho-Chunk (Winnebago), Peoria, and Kaskaskia Indigenous peoples. In 1885, Chicago, later known as the City of Big Shoulders, witnessed the construction of America's first skyscraper. The world's first Ferris wheel amazed visitors at the city's 1893 World's Columbian Exposition. Countless other inventions have been devised by our state's citizens—including the cell phone. No one knows exactly when Chicago's first deep dish pizza was baked, but it has become an Illinois institution and a national favorite. We are thirteen million people. We are proud. Together, we open the doors of the People's House to welcome you.

LEFT First Lady Mabel Kingston Green poses in a hat beside an airplane at the 1947 national aviation clinic held in Springfield. Mrs. Green was instrumental in supporting military efforts during World War II.

OPPOSITE A painting by Karl Wirsum, a graduate of the School of the Art Institute of Chicago, reflects the provocative and experimental approach of Chicago's Hairy Who group, of which Wirsum was a member.

FOLLOWING PAGES In the Governor's Dining Room, a folk-style mural created in 2019 by Chicago's Simes Studios depicts the life and landscape of Illinois, circa 1900.

ABOVE In the West Parlor, a bronze sculpture by John H. B. Storrs, born in Chicago in 1885, reflects the influence of his teacher Auguste Rodin, as well as the streamlined forms of the Art Deco movement.

OPPOSITE Artisans in the workshop of Mississippi Mud Pottery, located on the banks of the Mississippi River in Alton, Illinois, crafted the clay bluegills, the state fish, displayed in the ground-floor Reception Room.

I

THE
GOVERNOR'S
MANSION
TODAY

A NEW SPIRIT

On a cold and cloudy Wednesday in November of 2018, three weeks following JB's election, he and I walked up the long, curved drive to the house that was to become our home. We were excited to see the place that was known as the People's House, but to be honest, I felt a little overwhelmed as the reality of my new role was setting in. Michael Smith was also with us that day, and I am grateful that he was; his friendship, sunny disposition, depth of knowledge, and experience with important public homes, including a U.S. embassy and the White House, gave me confidence in my new role as caretaker of this great house. The mansion staff greeted us at the front of the door with a warm welcome, and I soon found out how important their combined decades of experience are to the success of running a governor's residence.

I knew the building had just been through a major renovation, but this was my first time seeing the finished project. As we walked through the house, I was impressed by the job First Lady Diana Mendley Rauner and the architects had done. It was only four years since Diana had come to the house as the wife of a newly elected governor and discovered that it was riddled with decay. Now all the plaster and woodwork of the rooms are pristine, and a new roof and windows will help protect the house. I realized how fortunate I was to benefit from their achievements. After the tour, I knew it was my job to continue the work they had begun and to finish the decoration of the house.

From the start, I understood that my mission was to create a hospitable environment for my husband's work as governor, a place that reflected his gregarious personality and love of people and where he could host events for legislators, visiting dignitaries, and, most important, the people of Illinois. That is why I turned to Michael, a student of history and architecture who knows how to create traditional interiors with an inviting, modern feel. Nothing about his work is cold or austere. Being in one of his rooms is like getting a hug. They are comfortable, but also correct and proper, and that reflects JB's mission and character. Michael brought that same approach, only more relaxed, to the family quarters, which are shared for the first time in these pages. These are the rooms where the governor and family retreat from the pressures of public duties.

The state rooms of the mansion are filled with things that had been collected and enjoyed by previous governors and their families—some of them possessing deep history. Michael showed these to best advantage by combining objects from many periods into a harmonious whole. Part of my vision was to fill the house with the work of Illinois artists, including modern and contemporary pieces. Some of these come from our personal collection and others are graciously loaned from the Illinois State Museum and the Abraham Lincoln Presidential Library and Museum. A few of my favorites are a 1938 self-portrait by surrealist Gertrude Abercrombie that hangs across the Music Parlor from a 2014 painting by Karl Wirsum of Chicago's Hairy Who group, and an 1860 portrait of a beardless Abraham Lincoln painted by Springfield artist Reverend Lewis P. Clover Jr. located in the Lincoln Parlor. The Greek Revival architecture of the interior proved a nimble frame for this wide variety of styles. Almost anything can find a home in a good classical interior.

One of my greatest joys has been working with the historic artifacts in the mansion's collection—portraits of the residents, the furniture they used, the china and silver with which they dined. The more I learned about these things, the closer I felt to those who had lived here before us and the prouder I became of their accomplishments. I feel as though I know them, as if they are all around me, guiding my journey. I hope I live up to their legacy.

Each room of the mansion and its contents has stories to share. Visitors ranging from students to tourists from out of state, Illinoisans, and dignitaries come to hear them speak of history. It is my hope that visitors and future first families will also cherish this house and its history and enjoy the results of this project, which was underwritten by private contributions—no public funds were used. With this book, I also hope to expand the mansion's reach by sharing the history of Illinois with those who have perhaps never visited the state. All proceeds from the sale of this book will go into the trust fund that supports the mansion's care.

PREVIOUS PAGES The gracious entry leading into the central hall is framed by columns that issue a stately invitation.

Wallpaper in a sepia edition of the 1812 Les Monuments de Paris pattern covers the walls of the first family's living room.

RIGHT The serene cream-and-gold color scheme of the West Parlor brings works by Illinois artists Evelyn Statsinger and John H. B. Storrs into high relief. A graduate of the School of the Art Institute of Chicago, Statsinger was recognized by Mies van der Rohe and contemporaries for her balance of abstraction with representation.

OPPOSITE A twin to the West Parlor across the entrance hall, the East Parlor shares the same wallcovering, mantel, and mirror. Its Recamier lounge and gilt over-mantel mirror introduce elements of nineteenth-century style to the timeless decor.

ABOVE A photograph from the 1920s shows the room's previous ornate plaster ceiling and cornice detail.

FOLLOWING PAGES The Music Parlor features a grand piano donated from the estate of John H. Johnson, publisher of *Ebony* and *Jet* magazines, that stands ready and waiting to entertain guests.

PREVIOUS PAGES Historic Lincoln artifacts adorn the walls of the Lincoln Parlor, including a framed letter from the president to Secretary of State William H. Seward that hangs beside a Lincoln portrait.

OPPOSITE AND ABOVE A nineteenth-century Russian gilt-bronze and glass chandelier forms a gossamer focal point amid the room's formal architecture while its cobalt-blue glass medallion offers contrast to the green walls.

LEFT Morning light illuminates the handsome Illinois black-walnut paneling of the library, which creates a perfect setting for a bust of Abraham Lincoln.

FOLLOWING PAGES During the 1971-1972 Ogilvie renovation, decorative arts expert Lowell Anderson and historian James T. Hickey found the three matching two-hundred-year-old Waterford chandeliers and the long table that grace the State Dining Room.

The mansion also acquired a voluminous ballroom during the same renovation and addition project. Pilasters inspired by those in the original entertaining rooms frame the windows and doors.

ABOVE A work in graphite
on paper by Chicago-
based artist David Klamen
combines precise realism
with atmospheric light.

OPPOSITE In *Faded Flag*, Black
American artist Theaster
Gates, who lives and works
in Chicago, created a
graphic composition using
decommissioned fire hoses.

ABOVE A portrait showing the beardless Lincoln in a rare, near-profile composition was painted circa 1925 by Chicago artist William Patterson. A great fan of the president, Patterson moved to Springfield from Chicago.

OPPOSITE The elliptical form of the two-story staircase allows for views from room to room and floor to floor. The pattern of the Adelphi Ornament and Stripe wallpaper echoes the shapes of the spindles and adds a vertical counterpoint to the staircase's wide curves.

FOLLOWING PAGES The Zuber & Cie wallpaper of the Kankakee Room is a replacement of the original wallpaper that was installed in the early 1970s. A secretary bookcase and cabriole-leg table from the mansion collection pay homage to past residents.

LEFT Michael Smith and First Lady Pritzker created the Chicago Room in celebration of Illinois design icons. With walls covered in Frances Elkins's signature tea paper, the room is furnished with reproductions of Elkins's twin canopied beds and a vintage Samuel Marx secretary cabinet (seen on the following pages).

ABOVE LEFT Born in Milwaukee, Frances A. Elkins (1888–1953) visited her brother, famed Chicago architect David Adler, in Paris when he was attending the École des Beaux-Arts. There she collaborated with interior designer Jean-Michel Frank and sculptor Alberto Giacometti. She worked extensively as a designer, often partnering with her brother on projects in Illinois and California. Her work is most widely known through the enduring popularity of her iconic Loop chairs, inspired by eighteenth-century French design.

ABOVE RIGHT Samuel A. Marx (1885–1964) was an American architect, designer, and decorator of the modernist school, influenced by the International Style. After graduating from the Massachusetts Institute of Technology, he studied in Europe. He practiced architecture in the Chicago office of the firm of Shepley, Rutan & Coolidge. His architecture has drawn comparisons to that of Mies van der Rohe, and his architectonic furniture follows suit in terms of its elegant minimalism.

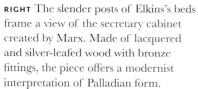

RIGHT The slender posts of Elkins's beds frame a view of the secretary cabinet created by Marx. Made of lacquered and silver-leafed wood with bronze fittings, the piece offers a modernist interpretation of Palladian form.

ABOVE The Chicago Room features silver pieces from the Kalo Shop, a group of artisans who began work in 1900 and became leading makers of Arts and Crafts silver. Its founders were six young women who trained at the Art Institute of Chicago and opened a retail shop in Chicago in 1914. The group gained renown for its fine silver flatware and holloware, as well as jewelry. The company flourished through the 1970s, producing work that evolved with the styles of the times.

LEFT The Ogilvie administration renovation of the mansion in the early 1970s included the creation of the Lincoln Bedroom, furnished with a bed and dresser said to have belonged to Lincoln, that was donated in 1969 by the estate of Herman L. Donovan, a past University of Kentucky president. Redecorated in 2022 by Michael Smith and First Lady Pritzker, the room includes a portrait of Governor Bissell on the left. The portrait on the right, likely painted by Stephen W. Shaw, depicts Edward Baker. A close friend of Lincoln and the namesake of his second son, Baker died in the Civil War. Friends of the president commissioned the portrait in 1861 and presented it to Lincoln in the White House. Mary Todd Lincoln gave it to the state in 1872.

FOLLOWING PAGES In the mansion's ground-floor Reception Room, a collection of miniatures hangs above the fireplace against custom-colored Adelphi Laurel Harlequin wallpaper. Its historic pattern complements their diminutive size. The green tones of the wallpaper and upholstery were inspired by the verdant colors of the mural in the adjoining Governor's Dining Room.

The Kankakee Room's Zuber
& Cie wallpaper in the Les Vues
d'Amérique du Nord pattern was
an inspiration for the mural in the
Governor's Dining Room. While
emulating the enveloping effect
of scenic wallpaper, this mural by
Chicago's Simes Studios celebrates
Illinois, depicting its topography,
towns, cities, farms, steamships,
and masted vessels. Some highly
detailed elements recreate the
appearance of late-seventeenth-

century wood-block production methods, but the techniques for others are drawn from folk art landscape painting. The panel above depicts steamships on the Mississippi River and a small farm. In the detail on the left, Chicago perches on a bluff above Lake Michigan with the Garden of the Gods rock formation on the left. The detail on the right pictures early Springfield, with the prominent dome of the capital city's first State House.

ABOVE A bull's eye mirror surmounted by an American eagle hangs above a cabinet in First Lady Pritzker's office.

RIGHT A supporter and collector of Illinois artists, with a particular interest in women, the first lady chose a postmodern abstract painting by contemporary Chicago artist Judy Ledgerwood for her office.

LEFT When in his office on the mansion's ground floor, Governor JB Pritzker works at a handsome partners desk flanked by U.S. and Illinois flags.

THE
FIRST FAMILY'S
QUARTERS

ABOVE A Regency-style
gilt- and ebonized-wood
framed mirror hangs above
a Federal mahogany settee
in the entrance hall.

OPPOSITE For the living
room, MK Pritzker chose
woodblock mural wallpaper, a
decorative feature popular on
both sides of the Atlantic in
the early nineteenth century.

RIGHT The wallpaper in the family quarters' entrance hall pays homage to Illinois's heritage of farming corn in an elegant manner with wallpaper in a late eighteenth-century French pattern entitled Empire dessin Maïs.

PREVIOUS PAGES A late nineteenth-century mirror in the Regency style hangs above the living room's marble mantel. Its carved giltwood and aqua-colored *verre églomisé* panels bring vibrant color and gold highlights to the room's muted palette.

LEFT A pair of maple spool beds juxtaposed against Adelphi Stars and Squares wallpaper with a geometric pattern create a more masculine environment for the Pritzkers' son's room.

ABOVE A bathroom featuring marble tile, a Venetian mirror, and 1930s-style glass-and-chrome sconces echoes the palette of the adjoining room.

OPPOSITE While the bold, repeating pattern of a Pierre Frey toile energizes the Pritzkers' daughter's room, the unified blue-and-white palette creates a serene retreat featuring a gessoed French-style bed.

OPPOSITE The bedroom of Governor and First Lady Pritzker offers calm respite from official duties with hand-painted Gracie Studio wallpaper in an 1898 Chinoiserie design and a canopied Regency poster bed.

ABOVE In the late 1950s, First Lady Dorothy Stratton had the mansion bedroom decorated with swagged chintz draperies in a floral garland pattern to balance the room's formality with femininity.

II

HISTORY
OF THE
PEOPLE'S
HOUSE

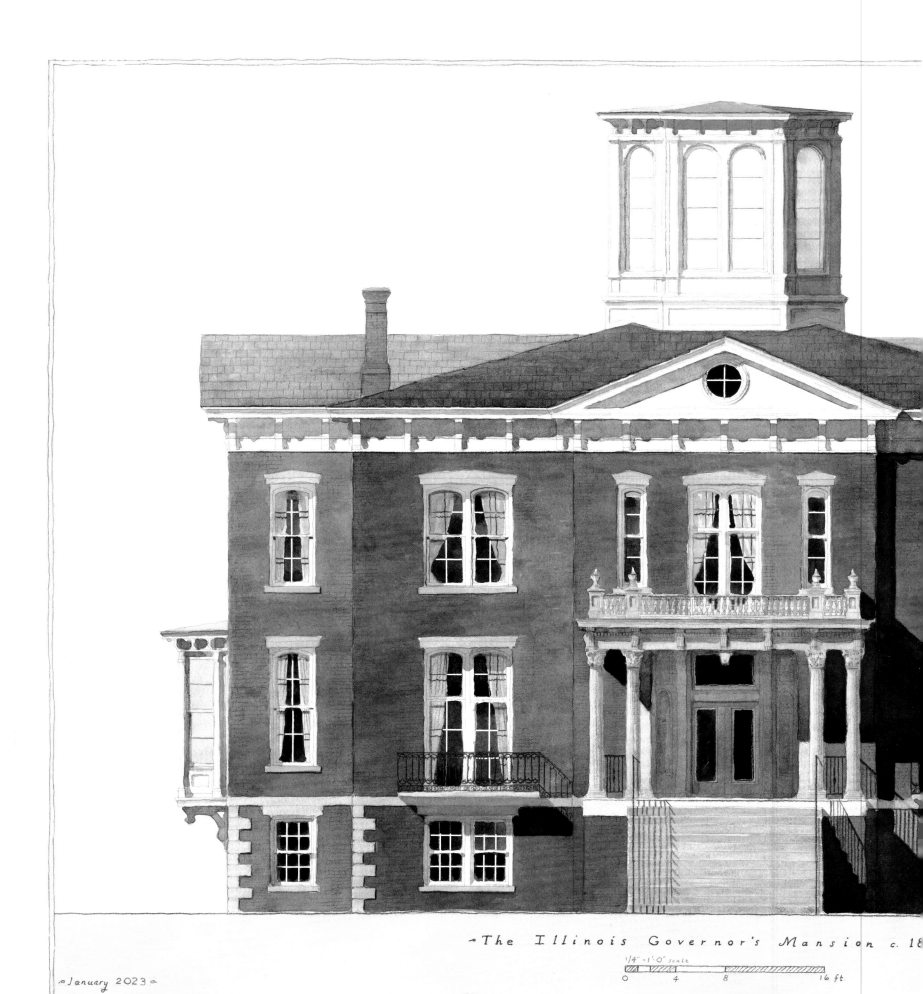

The Illinois Governor's Mansion c. 18

1/4" = 1'0" scale

0   4   8   16 ft

Rendered by: Martin Burns
Ferguson & Shamamian Architects

Today, nearly all of America's fifty states boast governors' mansions. Each is provided by the state to serve as the chief executive's residence and the site for social, political, and public functions. The history of these dwellings dates to the earliest of colonial times, beginning with the 1610 Spanish Palace of the Governors in what is today called Santa Fe, New Mexico. Reconstructions of two of the most magnificent can be found in the former British royal colonies, including the 1720 Virginia Governor's Palace at Williamsburg and the 1770 Tryon Palace in New Bern, North Carolina. These seats of colonial power were extravagant structures designed in the prevailing taste of the mother country. Those in the eastern colonies were built in the English Georgian style, which took cues from the work of sixteenth-century architect Andrea Palladio. Stately in symmetry and liberally adorned with features drawn from classical temples and civic buildings, this style has found favor in America's official buildings, including gubernatorial residences, for two centuries.

Following the American Revolution, the term "governor's palace" gave way to more democratic terms, such as governor's house, governor's mansion, and, later, executive mansion. While classical features, such as columns, pediments, and porticos, have remained prevalent, the manner of their expression has shifted over time, first to the neoclassical Federal style, next to the bold mid-nineteenth century Greek Revival style, then to the handsome Italianate aesthetic that enjoyed popularity in the latter part of the nineteenth century. All of these modes generally employed the language of classical architecture, flavored by the fashion of the day.

The Illinois Governor's Mansion, completed in 1855, combines elements from several of these styles—Georgian massing with pediments reminiscent of Palladio's villas, a portico and interior detailing in keeping with Greek Revival designs, and elements expressing the Italianate aesthetic. Since its construction in 1855, the house has undergone three major remodelings that have significantly changed its size and external appearance. Modifications to its interior design have occurred even more frequently, as most residing families introduced new furnishings, removing many

PREVIOUS PAGES A portrait of Richard J. Oglesby painted by George P. A. Healy in 1864 depicts the governor, a Civil War veteran, in a Union Army uniform.

LEFT In 2023, Ferguson & Shamamian Architects prepared this rendering of the front elevation of the Governor's Mansion as it appeared in 1855.

when they departed, and government appropriations were made to fund refurbishment and redecoration. While the frequency of such modifications may seem surprising, the constant usage of such dwellings for state, public, and personal gatherings, as well as for family living, made them necessary.

Illinois was admitted to the Federal Union as the twenty-first state on December 3, 1818, but it was not until twenty-five years later that a residence was designated to house Illinois governors and their families. In the meantime, governors were expected to provide housing at their own expense while residing in the capital. A bill calling for the purchase of a governor's residence was submitted in 1840 by State Representative Abraham Lincoln, but it was indefinitely tabled. It was not until 1843 that the state provided the first governor's residence—a modest two-story building formerly used as the office of the Board of Public Works. With cramped rooms, a front door opening almost directly to the sidewalk, a narrow front porch, and no yard for children, it quickly proved inadequate for political, social, and family functions. Another twelve years passed before a suitable building intentionally designed as a residence was constructed.

Once an adequate appropriation of funds was approved in 1853, building of the new Governor's Mansion, designed by prominent Chicago architect John Mills Van Osdel, commenced. Completed in 1855 with a grand facade, ornate and well-proportioned receiving rooms, and a spacious floor for family quarters, it promised to meet the various demands that would be placed upon it for years to come. Forty-two years passed before the first major renovation and reconfiguration of the mansion took place in 1897. The next significant changes occurred between 1971 and 1972 with the construction of a sizable addition, followed by another remodeling and landscaping program completed in 2018. From 2019 to 2022, under the Pritzker administration, a comprehensive redecoration of the mansion took place. Throughout all these changes, the original core of the house has remained intact. What follows is the story of the house, as told through the narratives of the people who lived in it, governed from it, cared for it, and preserved it for posterity. These accounts bear witness to the lives of those who resided in the Illinois Governor's Mansion and those who visited it and to the important events that transpired within its walls.

RIGHT A view of the East Parlor and adjoining Music Parlor, divided by ornate grillwork, documents the interior of the mansion as it appeared during Governor John P. Altgeld's administration (1893–1897).

EARLY DAYS
OF THE
GOVERNOR'S
MANSION
1855–1897

Joel A. Matteson
Mary Fish Matteson
(1853–1857)

In 1853, Governor Joel A. Matteson moved into the small house provided by the state with his large family, including his wife, Mary Fish Matteson, and their six children. A successful businessman, Matteson had moved in 1833 from New York to Illinois, where he became actively involved in endeavors promoting the development of the state, including the construction of the Illinois and Michigan Canal and several railroad lines. Respected for his business acumen, Matteson pursued a bold agenda as governor, promoting the expansion of railroads, the reduction of the state deficit, and the creation of a public school system. Soon after his inauguration, he announced in the *Illinois State Journal* that on Thursday evenings, from eight to eleven o'clock, he would host senators, representatives, state Supreme Court justices, and visitors to the city at the modest home. It quickly became evident that the building was unable to meet the demands placed upon it by Matteson's political life, as well as the needs of his family.

Soon after Matteson's term began, his colleague Senator Asahel Gridley—possibly at the governor's bidding—introduced a bill appointing a commission to build a new governor's residence. It was passed by the Senate and the House of Representatives in a single day, without debate. Five days later, Matteson signed the bill that called for the erection of a new "governor's house." As one of three commissioners appointed for the project, he supervised construction of the house and was undoubtedly intimately involved in every decision. The governor's daughter later wrote, "He seemed to have been given carte-blanche in regard to the building of it, and the consequence was that Illinois for many years had the finest executive mansion in the country. I can never forget the enormous entrance hall, widening half-way back, and the artistic staircase, winding up across the back in full view from the entrance."

The first order of business was to find an appropriate site. A piece of land called Cook's Grove was chosen and purchased for 4,500 dollars. Located four blocks from the square where the Capitol stood, the land was described in the *Illinois State Journal* as "elevated and . . . regarded as one of the best lots in the city." Among its attractions was its proximity to the stream known as the Town Branch that ran through it. Springfield resident Abraham Lincoln was said to have frequently fished in the Town Branch, where baptisms took place and children ice skated.

John Mills Van Osdel, Chicago's first professional architect, was chosen to design the mansion. His vision emulates several Palladian features, including the Renaissance-era architect's tripartite arrangement with a base, piano nobile, and mezzanine. Palladio's villas also favored the cruciform shape of Roman temples, which finds expression in the shallow pediments visible on all four sides of the mansion. These features, combined with the curved lines of the central stair hall, invite comparison to Palladio's masterpiece in Vicenza, the Villa Rotonda. Other details, particularly bracketed cornices beneath the eaves, windows shaped like tall, narrow Roman arches, and a central cupola, point to the Italianate style fashionable in the third quarter of the nineteenth century. The complex amalgam of styles also includes a Greek Revival portico with classical columns and pilasters with Tower of the Winds capitals.

Van Osdel's firm was a busy one, which may explain why Springfield-based builder Thomas J. Dennis played an active role in the design of the interior, fashioning many of its decorative details and devising a plan for the stair. While the Governor's Mansion's exterior is eclectic, the interior architecture adheres faithfully to the Greek Revival style with symmetrically disposed rooms featuring fluted columns and pilasters and robust yet austere cornices. As envisioned by Van Osdel, the plan of the first floor accommodated both small- and large-scale entertainments, with a grand hall leading to sizeable rooms divided by folding doors and pocket doors. These included four reception rooms, the State and

JOHN MILLS VAN OSDEL

The son of a Baltimore carpenter, John Mills Van Osdel (1811–1891) began working in the trade as a teenager after his father suffered from an accident. By the time Van Osdel was nineteen, he had created a successful school for prospective draftsmen. In 1836, Van Osdel met William Ogden, a New York State assemblyman and later mayor of Chicago, who invited him to design his Illinois residence. Upon completion of the Greek Revival house, Van Osdel stayed in Chicago, working on projects that included designing a bridge spanning the Chicago River and devising water pumps activated by a horizontal windmill for the Illinois and Michigan Canal program, for which he received the first patent ever issued to a Chicago citizen. In 1844, he opened Chicago's first architectural office and earned prominent commissions, including the Palmer House Hotel and Cook County Courthouse and City Hall. In 1853, he received a commission to design the Illinois Governor's Mansion. After the 1871 Chicago fire, Van Osdel's firm was flooded with projects, including some of the city's first fireproof buildings and the first thirteen-story building in the world. He is included in Chicago's pantheon of great architects alongside Daniel Burnham, Louis Sullivan, and Frank Lloyd Wright.

PREVIOUS PAGES Former Governor Matteson gazes into the distance with a thoughtful expression in an 1861 portrait by George F. Wright.

RIGHT The earliest known photograph of the mansion, taken circa 1860, reveals the Palladian cruciform shape of the structure, accentuated by shallow pediments on all four facades.

ABOVE The Tower of the Winds capital was chosen to crown the columns, pilasters, and pillars of the Governor's Mansion. The elegant form, which includes a single row of acanthus leaves surmounted by a row of long waterleaf motifs, became popular during the Greek Revival period, replacing the double-acanthus leaf form more associated with the Roman style. The capital's first use is traced to a meteorological tower constructed in the second century BCE, known as the Tower of the Winds. Like many elements popularized during the Greek Revival movement, it symbolizes the democracy associated with ancient Greece and imparts an air of stateliness and opulence to its surroundings.

THE GOVERNOR'S HOUSE (1855)

The design for the Governor's House, as it was originally called, dates from 1853, with construction completed in 1855. None of the original drawings from architect John Mills Van Osdel's design survive. Over seventy years of nearly undocumented changes occurred to the house before the earliest surviving floor plans were drawn in 1925. The plans on these pages are reconstructions based on research of the original building's internal masonry structure, inventories of room contents, contemporaneous first-hand accounts, and descriptions in newspaper articles, and are confirmed by the 1925 drawings. They represent a significant step toward solving the mystery of how the house originally appeared.

Built at a time when the neoclassical styles of the eighteenth and nineteenth centuries were giving way to the Italianate aesthetic, the mansion is eclectic in appearance. Elements of its original exterior are predominately Italianate, with arched windows, a low roofline, a bracketed cornice, and an octagonal cupola. This style, which gained popularity in the 1850s, derived from the architecture of rural Italian villas. The house also possesses classical features typical of the Greek Revival movement that shaped American architecture from the 1830s to the 1850s. These are expressed by the mansion's symmetry, the front portico supported by columns with Corinthian capitals, and shallow pediments capping the four wings of the building. The design of the house also hearkens to the architecture of Renaissance-era Italian architect Andrea Palladio, drawing comparison to his iconic Villa Rotonda, and to the eighteenth- and early nineteenth-century Georgian houses inspired by his villas. Many details within and without point to ancient Greece, serving as a metaphor for America's democratic ideals.

FIRST FLOOR PLAN

At the front of the house, a small formal entrance porch with classical features provided a place where the first family could greet guests and from which the governor addressed public gatherings on the lawn. This porch led into a spacious entrance hall that opened to four parlors connected by folding doors and pocket doors. These allowed the rooms to be used separately for small gatherings or opened to one another for entertaining on a grand scale. The parlors, which were adorned with Greek Revival–style interior architecture, included two square rooms with small balconies opening onto the front lawn and two larger rectangular rooms with polygonal window bays facing east and west. In addition, the first floor had two dining rooms, a larger one for state affairs and a smaller one for family meals and intimate occasions. Each of these opened onto a covered veranda. At the center of the house, a graceful elliptical staircase illuminated by the rooftop cupola ascended to the second floor.

SECOND FLOOR PLAN

Reached by the central elliptical stair, the private living quarters for the family contained six sleeping chambers. As on the first floor, each room offered ventilation, natural illumination, and views via tall window openings, bays, and verandas. In the second floor's central hall, the graceful lines of the curving stair descending to the floor below formed an elegant centerpiece. Two chambers opened directly to the central hall and the other four were reached by narrow corridors. The use of these rooms changed over time depending on the residing families' needs—they were employed alternately as family sleeping rooms, guest quarters, a nursery, and a private morning room. Smaller rooms opening off the larger chambers and hallways likely served as spaces to accommodate commodes, bathing rooms, storage, and dressing rooms.

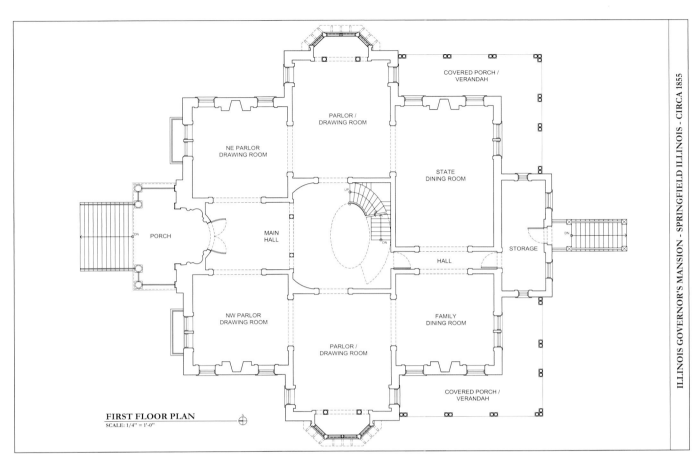

FIRST FLOOR PLAN
SCALE: 1/4" = 1'-0"

COVERED PORCH / VERANDAH

PARLOR / DRAWING ROOM

NE PARLOR DRAWING ROOM

STATE DINING ROOM

PORCH

MAIN HALL

STORAGE

HALL

NW PARLOR DRAWING ROOM

FAMILY DINING ROOM

PARLOR / DRAWING ROOM

COVERED PORCH / VERANDAH

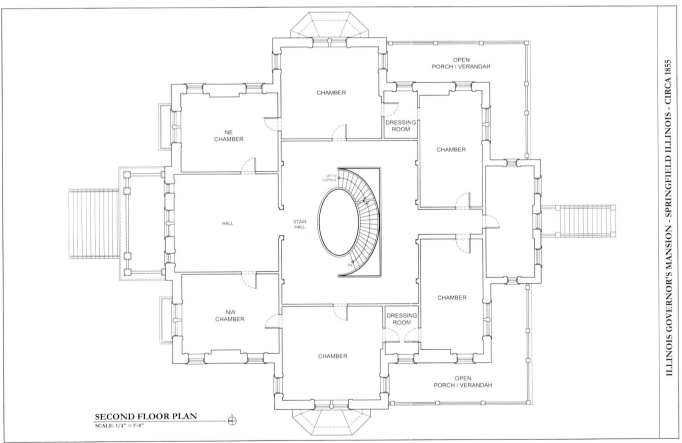

SECOND FLOOR PLAN
SCALE: 1/4" = 1'-0"

OPEN PORCH / VERANDAH

CHAMBER

DRESSING ROOM

NE CHAMBER

CHAMBER

HALL

STAIR HALL

UP TO CUPOLA

NW CHAMBER

CHAMBER

DRESSING ROOM

CHAMBER

OPEN PORCH / VERANDAH

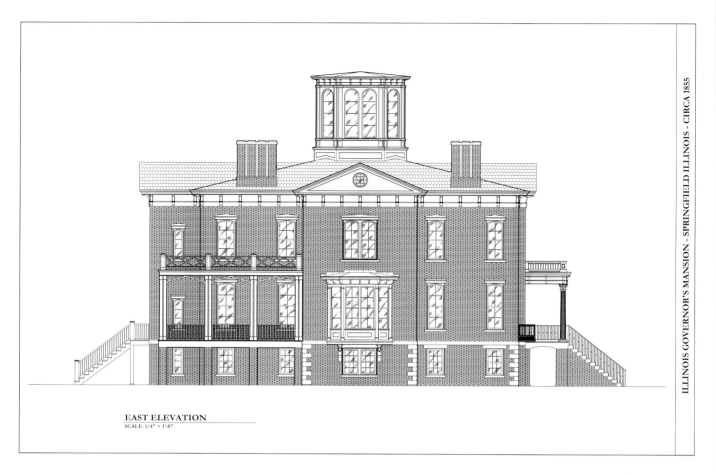

EAST ELEVATION
SCALE: 1/4" = 1'-0"

ABOVE An 1860 lithograph by H. G. Haerting, the first printed image of the mansion, documents architectural details later obscured or removed, including the cupola and one of a pair of rear porches.

GROUND FLOOR PLAN

Determining the exact plan and usage of the ground-floor rooms, which included areas for storage, others for heating and laundry, the kitchen, and servants' bedrooms, has proven challenging. The location of the exterior walls is known with certainty, but ideas of how the rooms were configured are based on clues and educated assumptions. This reconstruction is partially informed by a list of room items created in 1868 during the first Oglesby administration. Similar to the arrangement of the main floor, on the ground-floor rooms were arranged in a circular pattern around a central stair hall. Unlike the grand central stair of the main floor, the ground-floor staircase was likely a straight staircase designed for ease of use that connected the service rooms with the entertaining, dining, and private family rooms above.

ROOF PLAN

The attic space was located under a shallow pitched roof with an opening that channeled light from the fifteen-foot, octagonal cupola centered atop the roof into the formal stair hall below.

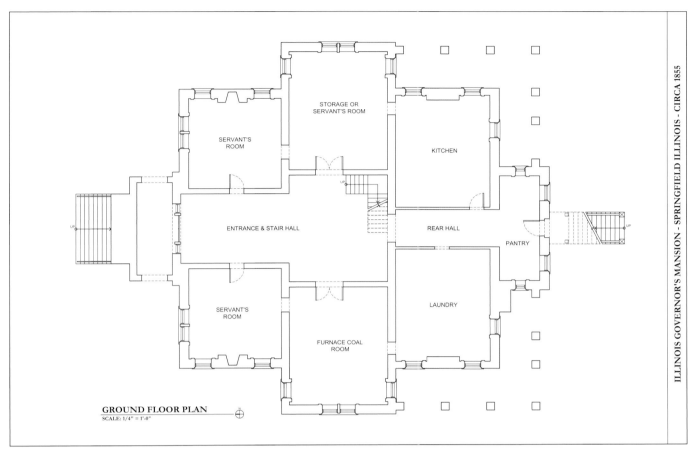

GROUND FLOOR PLAN
SCALE: 1/4" = 1'-0"

SERVANT'S ROOM

STORAGE OR SERVANT'S ROOM

KITCHEN

ENTRANCE & STAIR HALL

REAR HALL

PANTRY

SERVANT'S ROOM

LAUNDRY

FURNACE COAL ROOM

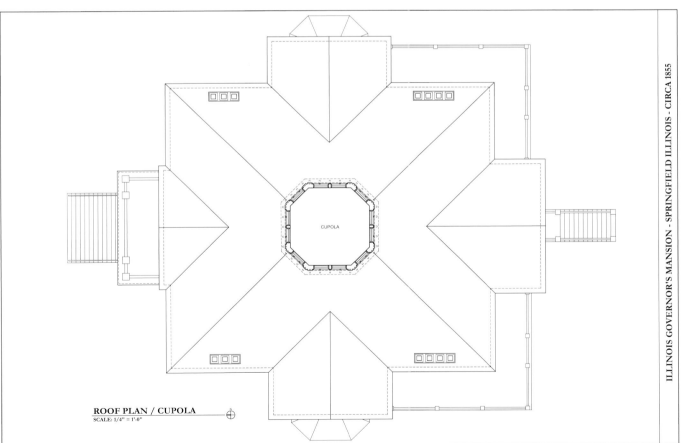

ROOF PLAN / CUPOLA
SCALE: 1/4" = 1'-0"

CUPOLA

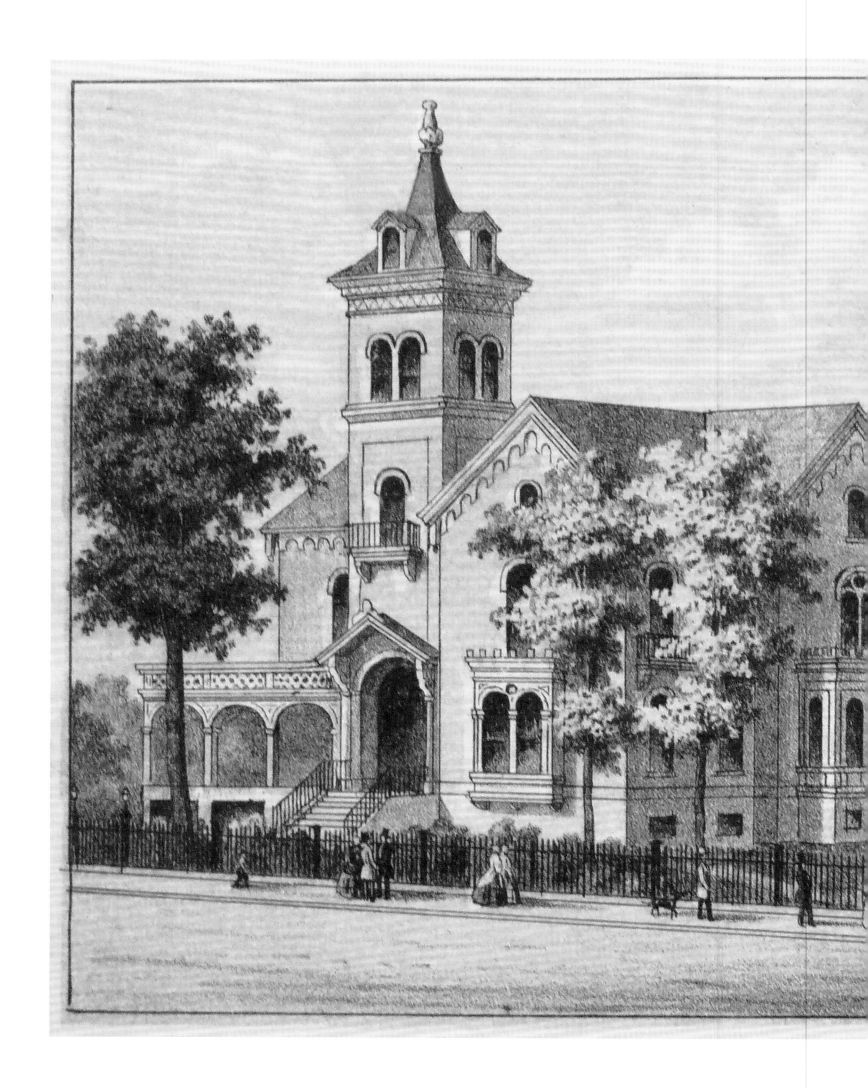

Family Dining Rooms, and a central hall with a sweeping, elliptical stair illuminated by the cupola.

Construction of the mansion began in 1853 and was completed in 1855. In November of that year, Governor Matteson and his family moved into their new home. The following January, the mansion opened to the public with a lavish reception. One thousand invitations were issued, and six hundred guests arrived to partake of a sumptuous supper followed by musical entertainment, dancing, and "promenading." The latter, which consisted of walking arm-in-arm with a partner, was a form of social interaction offered to those whose religion prohibited dancing. The party took place on an unusually cold evening, and the mansion's state-of-the-art gas system could not meet the challenge. Water froze in the gas lines, causing the lights to dim. However, candles were lit, the band played on, and festivities lasted late into the evening. The next day, the mansion opened to the public again, this time with a party for children.

LEFT An 1860 lithograph, also by H. G. Haerting, depicts the opulent, high-Victorian style house Governor Matteson built across the street from the Governor's Mansion following his term as governor.

ABOVE An 1862 portrait photograph taken in Paris shows Governor Matteson surrounded by his wife, Mary, and daughters.

Upon the end of his term, Matteson resolved to stay in Springfield, which he found to be a pleasant city with ample opportunities for the social life he enjoyed. Purchasing a lot across the street from the Governor's Mansion, in an area that came to be called Aristocracy Hill due to the prevalence of palatial houses, he commissioned an even grander residence designed by Van Osdel, reputed to have cost 100,000 dollars. Significantly larger than the mansion, it was designed in an aesthetic more in keeping with fashionable Italianate and Victorian-era styles. It eschewed previously popular classical details and instead featured scalloped trim along its steep gables and a tower with arched Italianate openings. Along with the Governor's Mansion, it was considered one of the finest buildings in town. In 1865, after Matteson vacated the house, colleagues of Abraham Lincoln proposed the idea of purchasing it and presenting it to him upon his retirement from the White House. It was said that when Lincoln was asked whether he intended to return to Springfield, he replied, "I expect to go back and make my home in Springfield for the rest of my life."

William H. Bissell
Elizabeth Kane Bissell
(1857–1860)

Governor Matteson's successor, William H. Bissell, served as a United States Representative from Illinois for three terms before being elected in 1856 as the state's first Republican governor. Bissell, who previously served as a physician, a colonel in the Mexican-American War, and a lawyer, entered politics as a Democrat. However, he became increasingly estranged from the party as it came to be dominated by Southern Democrats supporting a pro-slavery agenda. The passage of the Kansas-Nebraska Act, permitting slavery in those two territories, led to his renunciation of the Democratic party. His eloquent speeches about preserving the union and preventing the spread of slavery helped catapult him to success in the 1856 gubernatorial election.

A month after Bissell's inauguration, the new governor and his wife, Elizabeth Kane Bissell, presided over a "levee," as festive receptions were called at the time, which was glowingly reviewed in the *Daily Illinois State Journal*: "The supper tables, parlors and promenades all offered their full share of attractions. . . . A fine brass and string band discoursed most delicious music, and the dancers kept the cotillions filled until a late hour. Every body enjoyed the entertainment with more than ordinary relish." The governor and first lady shared the mansion with two daughters from Bissell's previous marriage and three of his wife's nieces, as well as Mary Koerner, the daughter of fellow statesman Gustave Koerner, who assisted the first lady with the busy social calendar. According to Mary, "Almost every evening there was company at the house, card-playing, dancing, and musical entertainment."

In addition to accommodating a full schedule of social and political gatherings, the mansion was the site of Governor Bissell's office because paralysis of the legs prevented him from traveling with ease to and from the State Capitol building. At the onset of his administration, he sought his colleague Abraham Lincoln's guidance, writing, "On getting to Springfield I shall desire to consult you as to what I shall say in my message to the Legislature about Kansas.

OPPOSITE The warm tones of Governor William H. Bissell's face, partially framed by crimson drapery, lend a vivid quality to this mid-nineteenth century portrait painted before he became governor in 1857 (artist unknown). Whereas most portrait painters of the period depicted sitters against dark backgrounds, the artist emulated a compositional element found in earlier likenesses of Founding Fathers, who often posed against red drapery. The painters of those portraits were, in turn, inspired by the Grand Manner portraits in Great Britain during the late eighteenth century. Bissell's pose exudes capability and confidence. Directed slightly away from the viewer, his gray eyes gaze into the distance with an expression of thoughtfulness. Surrounded by a fringe of dark hair, Bissell's luminous face appears both determined and benevolent. Leatherbound volumes painted beside his elbow, suggesting erudition, imply that he may be sitting in his library or office.

RIGHT Governor and First Lady Bissell were accompanied in the mansion by three of the first lady's nieces and the governor's two daughters from a previous marriage, including Rhoda Bissell, pictured here.

May I ask you to write out, hastily as you please, your views on that subject; that I may make such use of it as I deem proper in preparing my message?" Lincoln, acknowledged as a special advisor to Bissell, was a frequent visitor at the mansion for both official meetings and receptions. An 1895 account from the *Chicago Daily Tribune* describes him as having "a magic in his person that seemed to draw everybody to him, so wherever he went up and down the hall or the rooms were . . . groups to be broken up to let the crowd move on." Among Lincoln's private visits to the mansion was a meeting with Bissell during which one of the governor's nieces, Mary Kinney, locked them both out on the front porch. According to her account of the event, she left them there until they promised her "the best sack of candy that could be purchased in Springfield."

Early in 1860, Bissell's health declined when a cold turned into pneumonia. As he kept in bed, incapacitated by illness, Lincoln was returning to Springfield from New York, where he had delivered the Cooper Union address—a speech that propelled him toward the Republican presidential nomination. Rather than meeting with his friend and colleague to celebrate the event, as he anticipated, Lincoln found himself at Bissell's deathbed. The governor died the next day, on March 18, 1860. The Governor's Mansion was draped in black, and Bissell's body lay in state in the West Parlor, where thousands of citizens passed. An article in the *Chicago Press and Tribune* vividly describes the event, which was carried out in accordance with Bissell's Catholic faith: "The head was to the west, and at the head on either side the heavy crucifix burned the candles usual with the Church of Rome at such scenes. . . . The remains were dressed in a black suit, the figure entirely exposed, the top of the burial case being removed." Soon afterward, a sale of Bissell's personal property was held; among the items for sale was the governor's library of choice and valuable books. Bissell's successor, John Wood, permitted the first lady and family of young ladies to remain in the house for the remainder of the term, leaving his own family in Quincy, Illinois.

Richard Yates Sr.
Catharine Geers Yates
(1861–1865)

On January 14, 1861, Richard Yates Sr. became governor of Illinois amid the troubled times leading to the Civil War. Unlike Bissell, who was sworn in at the mansion due to his paralysis, Yates traveled in a military procession from the mansion to the State House, where he was sworn in with all due ceremony. By this time, the Governor's Mansion required refurbishment, so an appropriation was quickly made for improvements. Within the year, a favorable description from the *Missouri Republican* applauded the new decorations. "Rich Wilton carpets, velvet, of the medallion pattern . . . bedecked the floors, imparting an air of refinement and chaste elegance to the whole. . . . The windows were adorned with sweeping, heavy silk damask curtains, falling from massive gilt cornices, while full length mirrors in French glass, in

RIGHT In early 1861, shortly before Lincoln left Springfield for Washington, D.C., artist Thomas D. Jones (1817–1881) came from Ohio to model a bust from life. Despite his busy schedule, Lincoln posed for an hour a day for several weeks between Christmas of 1860 and February 1861 in a room at the Saint Nicholas Hotel. The work captures the mobility and animation of the subject's face more than many other depictions. The artist recalled that Lincoln was "a subject of great interest, but a very difficult study. His early mode of life and habits of thought had impressed hard and rugged lines upon his face, but a good anecdote or story, before commencing a sitting, much improved the plastic character of his features." Only a few copies of the bust were made, one of which was known to have been displayed in the mansion from at least 1896 through the 1920s. The copy seen here was donated to the mansion in 1972 by King V. Hostick of Springfield.

RIGHT In 1864, Wisconsin tradesman and marquetry master Peter Glass (1824–1901) crafted two tables to present to President and First Lady Lincoln. One of the pair, this tilt-top center table features an elaborate design fashioned from approximately twenty thousand pieces of wood, including holly, ebony, and some black walnut taken from fence rails said to have been split by Lincoln. Minute pieces of holly, stained in twenty-one varying shades, impart color to medallion portraits of Lincoln, Vice President Andrew Johnson, General Ulysses S. Grant, and General Benjamin F. Butler. Depictions of flowers, fruits, garlands, and eight different kinds of birds embellish the surface of the tabletop. In spring of 1865, Glass raised funds to transport the tables to Washington, D.C., by exhibiting them in Milwaukee and Chicago for a charge of twenty-five cents per viewing. The tables were still on display in Chicago when President Lincoln was assassinated. Glass later presented the works to Lincoln's son Robert Todd Lincoln, whose grandson Robert Todd Lincoln Beckwith donated this center table to the Governor's Mansion in 1976. It has been on display there ever since.

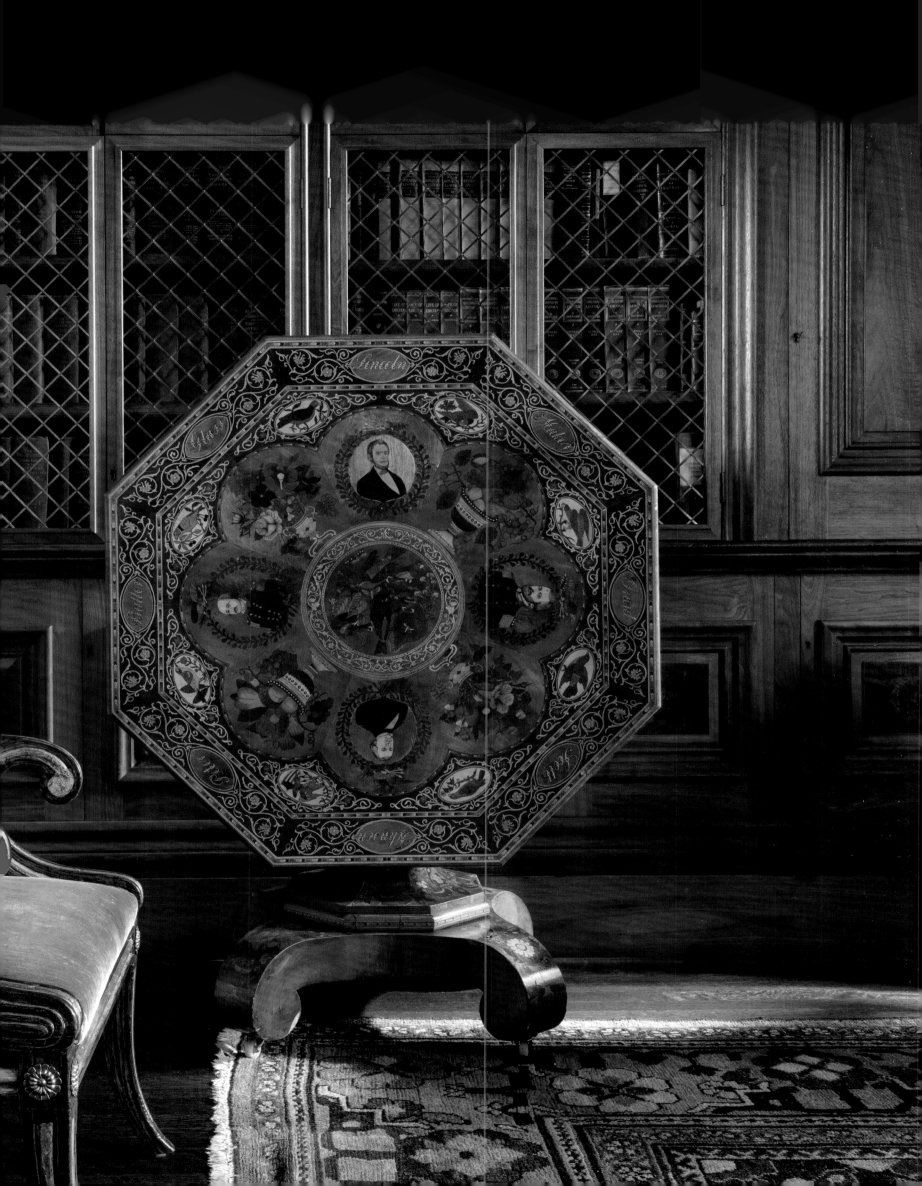

LEFT Popular and prolific American portrait artist George P. A. Healy (1813–1894) painted this likeness of First Lady Catharine Geers Yates, wife of Governor Richard Yates Sr., in 1865. Born in Boston, Healy studied in Europe and maintained a studio in Paris until he and his wife relocated to Chicago in 1856. Healy rendered portraits of cultural and political figures on both sides of the Atlantic, including Pope Pius IX, Franz Liszt, Henry Wadsworth Longfellow, and the presidents of the United States from John Quincy Adams to Ulysses S. Grant, for a project commissioned by the Corcoran Gallery of Art in Washington, D.C. His portrait of the beardless Abraham Lincoln was featured on a United States postage stamp. Yates's portrait was given to the state by the Yates family and has been on display in the mansion since 1949, on loan from the Abraham Lincoln Presidential Library and Museum.

ABOVE A hand-colored photograph of Governor Yates Sr. shows him seated with a serious demeanor, holding a scroll of paper in his hand.

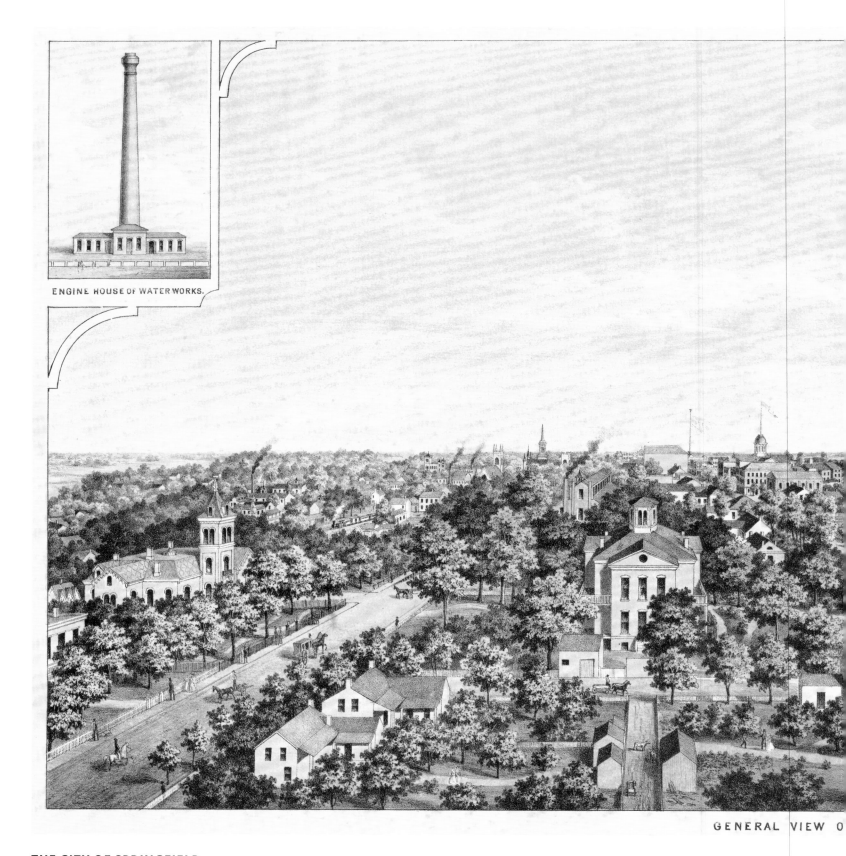

ENGINE HOUSE OF WATER WORKS.

GENERAL VIEW O

THE CITY OF SPRINGFIELD

Visiting Springfield to report about Lincoln's funeral, a special correspondent from the *New York Daily Tribune* penned a detailed account of the city, published May 8, 1865. "Springfield has a population of 15,000. It is the best-built small city I have ever seen. The private residences and grounds of the leading citizens indicate an opulence and tasteful elegance not to be found in many larger towns. It is laid out in wide streets, running with the cardinal points of compass, and covers immense ground for so small a population. Fifteen years ago, the State House (which is located in a public square in the very center of the city) was considered the finest structure in the West. The Executive Mansion, owned by the State, and occupied by the successive governors—now the home of Governor Oglesby—is certainly the finest gubernatorial residence in the country; spacious, excellent in architecture, and elegantly furnished. Some of the private residences are scarcely less elegant and imposing. That of ex-Governor Mattison[sic] is considered the best house in the State." In the above 1860 lithograph by H. G. Haerting, Matteson's mansion is located on the far left, the Governor's Mansion on the center left, and the old State House on the center right.

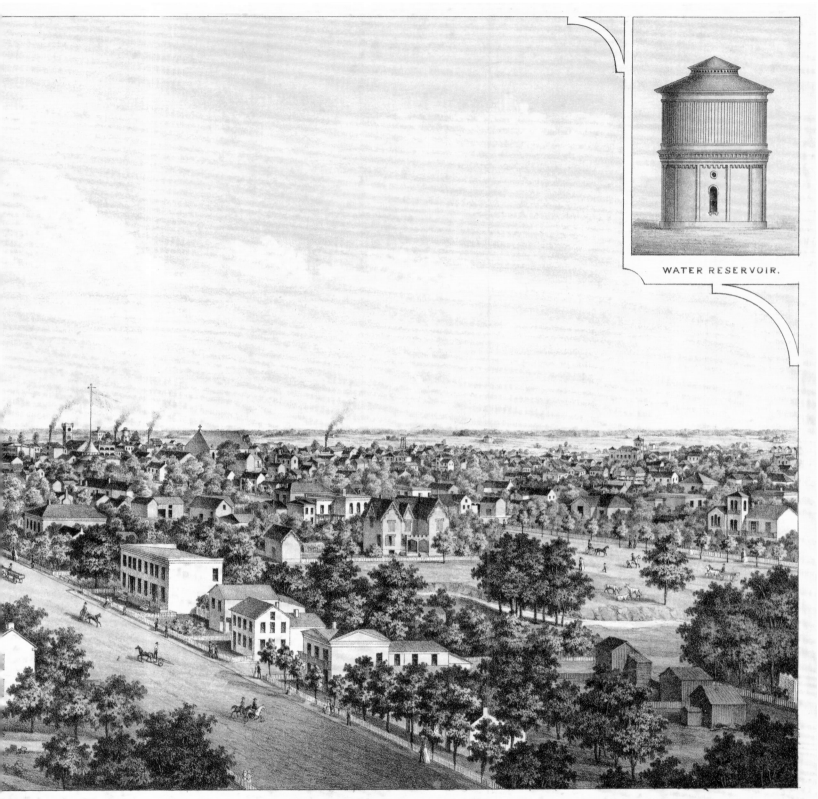

WATER RESERVOIR.

TY FROM SOUTH.

elaborate mouldings, doubled the brilliancy of every room. . . . The drawing rooms were not crowded with furniture. They were provided for convenience more than ostentation, with chairs and sofas in rosewood and brocatelle, and tables in rosewood and marble."

First Lady Catharine Geers Yates was a supportive wife who doubtless played a role in the decoration of the mansion and presided with grace over the many social engagements presented in its inviting rooms. An article chronicling one such event describes a supper served in one of the east rooms, furnished with a table in the form of a double cross replete with "boned turkeys and sugar-cured hams . . . aspiring pyramids of confectionary and fancy cakes, flanked by ponderous loaves of fruit, and pound, and sponge, frosted and adorned with all the cunning of the confectioner's art . . . with many flavored ice creams and many colored jellies, contributed to the luxury of the festive scene."

While a significant part of the refurbishment was devoted to rooms reserved for social and political gatherings, it also included areas devoted to official business. As the Civil War unfolded, Governor Yates spent many of his days and nights working in the mansion. It was from there that he wrote his patriotic war messages to the legislature. To keep up with profuse wartime correspondence, he maintained a clerical force in the house in addition to that at the State House. This employed three secretaries, including a night secretary whose duty was to answer as many of the "letters received by the bushel" as possible and assist "in the preparation of the more important state documents issued during the dark days of the Rebellion."

The war years were politically fraught in Illinois, where a unified campaign to defeat the Confederate army was marred by internal division. Still, Yates proposed to repeal a portion of the state's notorious Black Laws, which denied people with African ancestry basic rights. Known as the "soldier's friend," words engraved on his tombstone, Yates was tireless in his dedication to protecting living and wounded soldiers and to caring for the dead. In his memoir, the governor's son Richard Yates Jr. recalled his father striding up and down his room at night, "blue eyes either blazing with light or streaming with tears." Years later, he asked his father if this had really happened. "My father said, 'Yes, my son, those were the telegram nights. When I would receive word of a big battle, with thousands of Illinois boys wounded and killed, I could not sleep.

LEFT General Ulysses S. Grant visited Springfield in 1865 to honor Abraham Lincoln, whose remains were interred at Oak Ridge Cemetery. He stayed at the Governor's Mansion, then occupied by Governor Richard J. Oglesby, who served under Grant during the Civil War. He returned as president in 1874 for the formal dedication of the Lincoln Tomb. It appears that the reading copy of Grant's dedication speech, written on sheets of stationery headed "State of Illinois Executive Department," were prepared at the mansion. A circa 1900 bust of Grant by American artist Franklin Simmons (1839–1913) was donated to the Illinois Governor's Mansion Association in 1981. The work is modeled after the head of Simmons's marble statue of Grant displayed in the rotunda of the U.S. Capitol.

OPPOSITE When Richard Yates Sr. completed his term as governor in 1865, the Yates family donated a pair of opulent, gilded baroque-style mirrors to the mansion. Today they ornament the State Dining Room.

I used to walk the floor until morning.'" Yates's son also recalled his father hosting countless soldiers at the mansion. "On one occasion there were twenty at the table. I was told by a friend of Father's that, no matter whether the visitors were generals or privates, if they wore the uniform, he would ask them to stay to dinner—as many as the dining room could hold."

Richard J. Oglesby
Anna White Oglesby
(1865–1869)

Richard J. Oglesby was the first Civil War veteran to occupy the mansion. During the decades before his first term as governor, he also served in the Mexican-American War, made a successful foray to California during the Gold Rush, and, in 1860, won a seat in the Illinois state legislature. Oglesby proceeded to be elected three times as Illinois's governor, first in 1864, re-elected in 1872 for a term quickly cut short when he resigned to accept the position of U.S. senator from Illinois, then again for a second full term in 1884. Like Lincoln, he was born in Kentucky, and he is believed to have coined Lincoln's popular campaign nickname, the "Rail Splitter," reminding voters of his common-man origins.

Momentous events transpired during Oglesby's first year of service, including the second inauguration of President Lincoln in 1865. On April ninth of that year, the Civil War ended with Robert E. Lee's surrender at Appomattox, an event Oglesby marked two days later at the mansion by displaying the flag of the regiment in which he had served. Later that week while visiting Washington, D.C., he was received by Lincoln at the White House. That night, Lincoln was shot while attending a play at Ford's Theatre; Oglesby rushed to the Petersen House across from the theater, where physicians were tending to the fatally wounded Lincoln, and kept vigil with other officials and cabinet members.

After Lincoln's death, Oglesby was instrumental in planning his burial in Springfield and the funeral processional in which Lincoln's casket traveled by train from Washington to Springfield, making stops across the country so a grieving nation could pay its respects. The funeral cortège marched past the mansion on its way to Oak Ridge Cemetery for the final funeral service. After the funeral, Governor Oglesby and First Lady Anna White Oglesby presided over a reception for the state mourning delegations. Oglesby later served on the National Lincoln Monument Association that was charged with erecting a suitable tomb.

Other important events of Oglesby's first year in office included the ratification by Illinois of the Thirteenth Amendment abolishing slavery, which Illinois was the first state to adopt, and the long-sought repeal of many of the state's Black Laws. In September of 1865, General Ulysses S. Grant, under whom Oglesby had served, came to Springfield to pay homage to Lincoln. According to an article in the *Illinois State Journal*, the dignitary's visit was marked by a sumptuous dinner and reception at the mansion attended by a constant stream of guests who circulated among the four large parlors. Later that year, a procession of the 29th U.S. Colored Infantry marched by the mansion with colors flying and a band playing before a welcome-home gathering by local Black citizens at a nearby picnic ground.

Despite the seriousness of the times, the Governor's Mansion continued to serve as a center of Springfield social life, hosting levees that were attended with "avidity . . . [by] both citizens and strangers. For these events, the mansion was festooned with flags." One of the most festive of these events was the Grand Masquerade Party, deemed "one of the most fashionable and recherché events" of the season. But the year before Oglesby's first term ended, personal adversity struck the mansion when the first lady who had presided over so many solemn and festive events died of tuberculosis after being confined to her bed for a year. This was the second of two deaths bookending the governor's term, which began with the 1865 death of his five-year-old son Richard from diphtheria.

John M. Palmer
Malinda Ann Neely Palmer
(1869–1873)

Like Illinois's previous two governors, John M. Palmer was born in Kentucky. His father, an anti-slavery man, moved his family to Illinois, where Palmer attended college before selling clocks, teaching school, and practicing as a lawyer. During the Civil War, he fought for the Union, attaining the rank of major general. During the last year of the war, he served as Kentucky's military governor, commanding its federal forces, and helped to end slavery in the state. During the first year of his term as Illinois governor, he presided over the seventh anniversary of Emancipation Day, delivering a speech supporting the civil rights of Black Americans. This event in Springfield was honored by a crowd of two thousand people who marched past the mansion and Lincoln's former home on the way to the late president's grave at Oak Ridge Cemetery.

OPPOSITE Clockwise from upper left: Governors Richard J. Oglesby, John M. Palmer, John P. Altgeld, and Joseph W. Fifer.

In contrast to the tumult of the previous years, Palmer's term as Illinois's governor was a relatively peaceful one. An 1870 census shows that he was accompanied in the Governor's Mansion by a large family, including his wife, Malinda Ann Neely Palmer, and six children aged two to sixteen. Although the first lady suffered from tuberculosis, one of their daughters was blind, and a son was epileptic, the family regularly opened their home to statesmen and civilians alike. One of the most lighthearted affairs was the reception of visiting baseball teams at a time when baseball was becoming a popular sport in Springfield and beyond. Recalling these early years of the sport, a 1937 article recounts, "Originally . . . baseball had its high social side. In Springfield, the first ball teams were formed in the first rank of our blooded families."

Among the most noted statesman to visit the mansion was orator, abolitionist, and social reformer Frederick Douglass, who visited Springfield in 1872 to deliver an address. Afterward, he attended a reception at the mansion, where he was "cordially received by Governor Palmer" and introduced to prominent statesmen and citizens. An account of the event in the *Illinois State Journal* describes a "smiling, happy, cheerful crowd" in "brilliantly lighted parlors," drawing stark comparison with the statesman's reception later at a hotel in Saint Louis, where he was denied entry to the dining room.

Tragedy struck during Palmer's term in 1871 with the Great Chicago Fire. Abetted by the predominant use of wood as a material for buildings and sidewalks, and drought conditions, the fire destroyed nearly a third of the city and left close to 100,000 people homeless. In the weeks that followed, homeless citizens sought shelter in public buildings and martial law was enacted to patrol the streets and protect the warehouses holding relief supplies. An outpouring of money, food, clothing, and other necessities flowed in from across the United States and abroad. From the mansion, Governor Palmer penned a call for a special session of the General Assembly to provide relief. He also strongly protested the use of federal troops to keep order without their having been requested by the governor.

Richard J. Oglesby
Emma Gillett Keays Oglesby
(1885–1889)

In 1885, Richard J. Oglesby began his second full term as governor of Illinois, accompanied by his second wife, Emma Gillett Keays Oglesby, daughter of a local cattle baron. In contrast to his first term, which was overshadowed by Lincoln's assassination, Oglesby's next began peacefully. Once more, conditions at the mansion required attention, and government funds were drawn upon to install new sidewalks and limestone coping, described as "an added ornament to the mansion," and to build a new wing. Attached to the south side of the house, the addition accommodated a ground-floor laundry room, first-floor kitchen and serving area, and bedrooms above. The work was completed in time for

OPPOSITE In 1860, American artist Lewis P. Clover Jr. (1819–1896), also a reverend and citizen of Springfield, painted a portrait of Abraham Lincoln. The result of four or five sittings, the work depicts the beardless statesman in a thoughtful pose. Clover later wrote, "No man . . . could stand higher in all that constitutes the faithful husband, father, and citizen, and none more honoured and beloved than Abraham Lincoln." Born in New York City in 1819, Clover was the son of an art supply purveyor and publisher of prints. In his teens, he apprenticed under Hudson River School painter Asher Durand and exhibited at the American Academy of Fine Arts. He later showed works at the Boston Athenaeum, Pennsylvania Academy of the Fine Arts, and Philadelphia Art Association. The painting is on loan from the Abraham Lincoln Presidential Library and Museum. The circa 1815 Baltimore pier table beneath the painting stood for decades in the West Parlor at Mount Vernon. Fashioned from Honduran mahogany, the piece features gilded dolphins and ball feet. It was likely among a selection of objects donated by Chicagoan Mary Leiter to furnish Mount Vernon in the 1870s when the Mount Vernon Ladies' Association renovated the house, inviting interested individuals or groups from different states to "adopt" rooms. When decoration of the Illinois Room stalled, Leiter purchased many objects at her own expense. After Mount Vernon deaccessioned the table in 1994, it entered private hands, where it remained until sent to auction in 2019 and purchased by First Lady MK Pritzker to donate to the mansion.

EMMA GILLETT KEAYS OGLESBY

Governor Richard Oglesby's second wife, Emma Gillett Keays Oglesby (1845–1928), was the daughter of John Dean Gillett, a wealthy Illinois cattle baron. After American artist Franklin Tuttle completed portraits of her parents, he was commissioned to paint likenesses of the governor, his wife, and their children. For her portrait with her son Jasper, the first lady wore a silk-satin coat trimmed with ermine in the manner of European royalty, who adopted the rare fur as a symbol of power and wealth. A ruby-encrusted cross reminiscent of royal jewelry further enhanced her costume. Tuttle also painted a likeness in which sons John and Richard wear satin suits with lace collars in the style of seventeenth-century Charles II Restoration England and hold paddles and shuttlecocks. An anglophile who admired and imitated the social customs of Great Britain, the first lady was known for lavish entertainments, including a Dickens Reception in which "the spacious parlors were a mass of moving queer and antique costumes," with characters from the author's novels represented.

"THE FIRST DYNAMITE BOMB THROWN IN AMERICA"

THE PERSONNEL OF THE GREAT ANARCHIST TRIA[L]

BEGUN MONDAY JUNE, 21 ST 1886 . ENDED FRIDAY, AUGUST, 20 TH 1886 .

Attention Workingmen!

GREAT
MASS-MEETING
TO-NIGHT, at 7.30 o'clock,
AT THE
HAYMARKET, Randolph St., Bet. Desplaines and Halsted.

Good Speakers will be present to denounce the latest atrocious act of the police, the shooting of our fellow-workmen yesterday afternoon.

THE EXECUTIVE COMMITTEE.

Achtung Arbeiter!
Große
Massen-Versammlung
Heute Abend, halb 8 Uhr, auf dem
Heumarkt, Randolph-Straße, zwischen Desplaines- u. Halsted-Str.

☞ Gute Redner werden den neuesten Schurkenstreich der Polizei, indem sie gestern Nachmittag unsere Brüder erschoß, geißeln.

Das Executiv-Comite.

THE HAYMARKET AFFAIR

On May 3, 1886, two Chicago men were killed by police during a labor demonstration in support of an eight-hour workday. The next day, hundreds of people gathered in Chicago's Haymarket Square to protest the deaths. Near the close of what began as a peaceful event, an unknown person threw a bomb at the police who were attempting to disperse the crowd. The bomb and ensuing gunfire left seven policemen and an unknown number of attendees dead. In the trial that followed, seven men accused of complicity in the bombing were convicted and sentenced to death; another was sentenced to a prison term of fifteen years. Four of the condemned were hanged, one committed suicide in jail before the hanging, and two death sentences were commuted to life imprisonment by Governor Richard J. Oglesby. Seven years after the riot, Governor John P. Altgeld pardoned the surviving defendants and criticized the bias of the trial. The Haymarket Affair is considered a crucial event in the workers' rights movement. It is widely acknowledged as the origin of International Workers' Day on May 1, the day the general strike that ended in violence began.

Christmas festivities that included a pre-holiday gathering for children where several hundred coasted on the snowy lawn. Children were also invited into the life of the mansion on Christmas day, with a "Christmas-tree for the little folks, which the Governor's family never omits." A reporter from the *Chicago Daily Tribune* wrote that the mansion rang with the laughter of children and the governor "rollicked among the little folk like a boy."

In 1886, Chicago's Haymarket Affair, a peaceful protest for workers' rights that turned deadly, shocked the people of Illinois. Several policemen and many civilians were killed, and eight men were accused of, tried for, and convicted of complicity in the bombing, with seven sentenced to death. During the year that followed, Oglesby reviewed hundreds of letters that arrived about the incident and trial and ultimately commuted the death sentences of two of the men to life in prison.

In April 1888, the governor and his wife observed the state's first Arbor Day, during which trees honoring each governor were planted on the grounds. In July of that year, guests were invited into the mansion to admire the work of well-known artist Franklin Tuttle, who exhibited portraits he had painted of the first lady's parents and other works in the mansion's parlors, where they were greatly admired. Tuttle proceeded to spend the better part of three months at the mansion painting a series of portraits, including several of the governor, his wife, and their children. In 2015, one of the portraits, marred by tears and flaking paint, was discovered in the mansion's basement. Now restored, it hangs in one of the mansion's original bedrooms.

Joseph W. Fifer
Gertrude Lewis Fifer
(1889–1893)

Joseph W. Fifer was born in Virginia but at the age of sixteen moved with his family to Illinois, where he attended public schools and worked in his father's brickyard. During the Civil War, he served in the Illinois infantry, from which he was honorably mustered out after being severely wounded in General Ulysses S. Grant's Vicksburg campaign. Following the war, he established a legal career before entering public service as a city attorney, a state attorney, and for two terms a state senator. In 1888, he was elected governor of Illinois. During his term, he signed legislation founding the state historical library, reforming schools and election procedures, and granting women the right to vote for school officers. In July of 1890, he observed the funeral of Robert Gorum, a Black citizen who served over sixteen years as a gubernatorial messenger, by ordering the closure of executive offices. In Gorum's obituary in the *Chicago Inter Ocean*, he is described as having "a more extensive acquaintance among the politicians and public men than any other colored man in the State."

By the time Fifer and his wife, Gertrude Lewis Fifer, moved into the mansion, repairs to the interior were required. A newspa-

FREDERICK DOUGLASS
Renowned abolitionist, social reformer, statesman, and orator Frederick Douglass (1818–1895) spoke in Springfield several times. In 1872, he was welcomed by Governor John M. Palmer to the Governor's Mansion at a public reception, where he was introduced to prominent members of state. By this time, Douglass was widely known for his eloquent speeches. Formerly an enslaved person, he won his legal freedom in 1846 when British admirers purchased him from his former owners and formally released him from slavery. Long before he was emancipated, Douglass traveled widely in America and Great Britain, speaking in favor of abolition and suffrage for Black people and women. In 1848, he was the only Black person to attend America's first women's rights convention in Seneca Falls, New York. He came into contact with the highest leaders of state, including Abraham Lincoln, with whom he met three times. Among the most photographed men in the nineteenth century, he embraced photography as a democratic art form providing a means to publish realistic representations of Black persons that countered the demeaning stereotypes printed in both Northern and Southern publications. At a time when the field of photography was nearly exclusively male dominated, Douglass sat for Chicago-based photographer Lydia Cadwell for at least three portraits in 1875.

OPPOSITE A nineteenth-century banjo clock with a hand-painted scene of Mount Vernon is part of a collection of objects given by noted philanthropist John M. Olin to Southern Illinois University at Edwardsville and loaned to the Governor's Mansion in 1976.

perman from the *Chicago Tribune* described its dire condition, writing, "It has stood as a relic of ante-bellum days. Its walls were dingy with age, ceilings were cracked and about to fall, . . . [and] sewer gas pervaded every apartment. . . . [I]t was about as uninviting a place to be selected for the place of habitation for a human being as could be found anywhere." The Fifers' children, however, were unperturbed by the decrepitude of the house, as illustrated by recollections of their daughter, Florence, who was twelve at the time of her father's inauguration. In her account, she remembered, "The great spiral stairway probably impressed me more than anything else inside the mansion as it would any child who loves sliding down banisters. The first opportunity to try it out came the next evening. The children were all expected to remain upstairs during the inaugural ball. To the consternation of everyone, we came sliding down into the midst of the reception line scattering dignitaries to the right and left."

"During those earlier years, the mansion was the center of much social life in Springfield," Florence wrote. "This was before the days of hotel ball rooms and assembly dances, and so . . . [t]he state dining room was the scene for many a gay cotillion." Despite the gaiety of mansion entertainments, the house's dilapidation called urgently for repair and redecoration. "In the parlors the ceilings are patched and long screws with heavy plates hold the plaster in place," wrote a reporter for the *Chicago Inter Ocean*. "The family and state dining rooms back of the parlors are in worse condition. The once handsome mahogany doors have lost their graining in many places until they are as spotted as a leopard skin. . . . The walls of these rooms are covered with dark paper, which . . . is now sadly out of date, and the paper has been on so long that it has loosened from the walls and in places is ready to fall off." Proceeding to the second-floor bedrooms, the writer observed, "The walls are covered with even darker and dingier paper than those in the rooms below. The paint is scaled off the woodwork, and the old-fashioned inside window blinds make the rooms look more like APARTMENTS IN AN ASYLUM or prison than the home of the Governor."

By March of 1889, a committee had made a full inspection of the mansion, and in May, Fifer approved appropriations for repairs and refurbishment. To avoid the appearance of partisanship, he appointed three commissioners to oversee the work—a Springfield businessman, a hotel operator, and a newspaperman known to be a Democrat. The three consulted with the first lady concerning every aspect of decoration and refurnishing. When rehabilitation commenced, many contents of the mansion were removed, including portraits of former governors that were transferred to the State House. Architect George H. Helmle, son of a German-trained woodcarver, and painter and decorator George Schanbacher were hired to direct the project with the aid of a host of workmen. Among these were plasterers Rogers & Lott, who redecorated the ceilings with new centerpieces, brackets, and ornamental work. By the time the project was completed eight months later, it was said that thirty men were constantly employed.

VACHEL LINDSAY

One of America's best-known poets of the early twentieth century, Vachel Lindsay (1879–1931) grew up across the street from the Governor's Mansion. A childhood friend of Florence Fifer, Lindsay visited the Governor's Mansion frequently during the Fifer administration as well as during John P. Altgeld's term and made readings and performances of his work at the mansion for the Lowden family. Lindsay studied at the School of the Art Institute of Chicago and the New York School of Art before finding his voice as a poet. In 1905, he printed a pamphlet entitled "Rhymes to Be Traded for Bread" and traveled from New York to Florida, Kentucky, Ohio, Illinois, and New Mexico, trading self-printed poems for victuals and lodging. Intrigued by the ancient Greek idea of poetry as sung or spoken word, he referred to his work as "singing poetry," and considered himself a modern troubadour performing what he called "higher vaudeville." His subjects were vividly American, with verses depicting small town and rural White and Black American experiences. Springfield, its citizens, and its leaders inspired several poems, including "Abraham Lincoln Walks at Midnight," "Lincoln," and "The Eagle That Is Forgotten."

OPPOSITE Pictured in 1919, American poet Vachel Lindsay is acknowledged for his many contributions to the art of oral poetry. The city of Springfield, its citizens, and its leaders inspired many of Lindsay's poems, including "Lincoln," in which the poet exclaims, "Would I might rouse the Lincoln in you all!" In his poem, "The Eagle That Is Forgotten," Lindsay eulogizes Governor John P. Altgeld, extolling his integrity and bravery in the Haymarket rioters' pardons.

FLORENCE FIFER BOHRER

Florence Fifer (1877–1960) was the eldest of Governor Joseph Fifer and First Lady Gertrude Fifer's three children. A lively child, she kept an alligator in a fountain on the mansion's porch and rode her pony up the front steps. Florence also played an active role as hostess at the mansion's youth-oriented events. After marrying attorney Jacob Bohrer in 1898, she founded the Mother's Club, which eventually merged with the Parent-Teacher Association, and focused her attention on such issues as childhood tuberculosis and the shortage of sanitariums. In 1924, only four years after the ratification of the Nineteenth Amendment, she became the first woman to be elected to the Illinois State Senate. Florence served two terms, during which she promoted the training and licensing of midwives, child welfare, public safety, and the creation of Illinois's state park system. Following her time in the senate, she became chairperson of the McLean County Emergency Relief Fund, which provided aid during the Depression, founded and presided over the McLean County League of Women Voters, and was elected to the board of the National League of Women Voters.

OPPOSITE The elliptical staircase at the heart of the mansion creates a design statement that is both graceful and dramatic. As a child, Florence Fifer slid down the banister during her father's inaugural ball.

In December of 1889, a reporter from the *Illinois State Journal* wrote approvingly of the updated interior decoration in which heavy Greek Revival moldings had been replaced with "more modern 'grill,' or 'fretwork,'" and the parlors and the halls frescoed in delicate colors. "The appearance is further improved by the new carpets and window draperies that are combined in the general color scheme to give a suitable effect and harmony of color and design." Improvements were also made to the executive office and library, where walls were painted in mahogany tones in the former and blue in the latter, with a decorative lattice frieze featuring a stylized clematis vine with blossoms. The governor's quarters also included a private sitting room furnished in pink plush. With his time at the executive office taken up largely by callers, these were the rooms where Governor Fifer transacted the greater portion of his work and signed his name to state papers of importance.

The mansion's plumbing fixtures also received an upgrade during the renovation, including installation of an "open lavatory washstand of new style with elegant marble top and heavy silver-plated water fixtures, and two magnificent porcelain-lined Roman bath tubs." The project also included other, more critical improvements to the sanitary conditions with the installation of a connection to the city sewer. Previously, the mansion had no sewer connection, relying instead on cesspools. These emitted dangerous gases that may have contributed to the ill health of some of the occupants. It is likely that modern toilets powered by a gravity-driven cistern system located in the attic may also have been installed, as was common in affluent homes at that time.

A dramatic change to the outward appearance of the mansion occurred when its brick exterior was painted a lighter tone inspired by the White House. According to an 1889 article in the *Illinois State Journal*, "The building . . . now appears in a light stone color, which relieves the ponderous structure and gives it a more modern character." By 1890, the work was complete, and the governor and first lady celebrated with a dinner for the members of the commission who managed the project and their wives. Later that month, the Fifers held their first reception in the redesigned mansion, affording the public an opportunity to see its refitting. At the time, the *Chicago Inter Ocean* announced, "Governor and Mrs. Fifer are to be congratulated on beginning the new year of 1890 in an elegant home, instead of a barn as last year."

John P. Altgeld
Emma Ford Altgeld
(1893–1897)

John P. Altgeld, the first Democrat to occupy the mansion since 1857, governed the state of Illinois during a time of profound social change, particularly in the arena of workers' and women's rights. A leading figure of early progressive reform, Altgeld supported and signed some of the nation's earliest workplace safety and child labor laws. Equally ahead of his

ABOVE In her wedding photograph, First Lady Gertrude Lewis Fifer wears a fashionable late nineteenth-century style dress with muttonchop sleeves and a corseted waist.

LEFT The Music Parlor as it looked in 1897 with a two-tiered gasolier and elaborately carved tables and chairs. The room had been redecorated by First Lady Fifer, and remained unchanged during the Altgeld administration.

time, he appointed women to important roles in state government. Increasing funding for public education in Illinois, he also demonstrated a commitment to the widespread accessibility of education. Altgeld was a persuasive orator whose public speeches drew hundreds of people and a prolific writer who penned pleas for social justice, excoriated greed and corruption, and called attention to the inhumane conditions at the Cook County Insane Asylum.

Even before he became governor, Altgeld was deeply concerned about the fate of the three surviving defendants in the Haymarket Affair case, whom he believed had been unfairly tried, convicted, and sentenced. After lawyer Clarence Darrow and others petitioned him, Altgeld pardoned them, issuing a statement from the mansion containing a ringing condemnation of the prosecutor, the judge, and the jury that had found them guilty. While applauded by labor supporters in America and around the world, his actions drew intense opposition. Considering that Altgeld suffered from ill health, this willingness to address controversial social problems is all the more remarkable. Plagued by insomnia and a variety of physical ailments, he also suffered from a nervous disposition that resulted in a breakdown following the execution of four of the Haymarket defendants in 1887.

First Lady Emma Ford Altgeld was also a social activist and she hosted many meetings and events supporting the work of progressive organizations. An advocate for women's rights, she supervised the formation of the Springfield Woman's Club and held regular gatherings of the group. In addition to discussing social, economic, and political issues of concern to women, the group invited female activists to report on the work of social service groups, such as the Salvation Army. In May of 1895, the Altgelds hosted a reception honoring the Illinois Women's Exposition Board, which was in town to present to the state a statue by sculptor Julia M. Bracken called *Illinois Welcoming the World*, still prominently displayed in the State Capitol building. Other events included a reception for the Illinois State Teachers Association and one for attendees of a conference on charities and corrections. At the latter, the orchestra of the Illinois School for the Blind in Jacksonville performed.

Throughout his term, Altgeld suffered from illness, possibly caused in part by the unresolved chronic unsanitary conditions in the mansion. However, he chose not to request appropriations to improve these problems, citing his commitment to fiscal responsibility. In 1898, a writer for the *Chicago Inter Ocean* recalled that the house had been barely habitable in Altgeld's time. "There was constant danger . . . of the explosion of the boiler," he wrote. "It was so far gone that it could not stand sufficient pressure of steam to heat the house." In addition, he reported that the earth beneath the basement was soaked with sewage. "In the light of what the workmen developed last summer in digging under the basement floors, it is small wonder that Governor Altgeld took frequent trips for his health, and he can thank the god of Democratic economy that he didn't die of some new brand of malarial fever before he finished his term."

OPPOSITE Renowned Chicago-based artist Ralph E. Clarkson (1861–1942) received a commission to paint Governor John P. Altgeld in 1898. A Massachusetts native, Clarkson began his artistic training in 1881 at the School of the Museum of Fine Arts in Boston before continuing his studies in Paris at the Académie Julian. By 1889, Clarkson had returned to the United States, where he began working in New York City while making trips to Europe to paint. During that time, he received commissions for the World's Columbian Exposition in Chicago. In 1895, he established his studio in Chicago, due to the ample opportunities for portrait painting, and became the center of a group of notable artists there. In 1909, he was among the first members of the Cliff Dwellers club, a private civic arts organization housed in Chicago's Orchestra Hall whose members included architect Frank Lloyd Wright and landscape architect Jens Jensen. Clarkson also taught painting at the National Academy of Design and the School of the Art Institute of Chicago. The portrait is on loan to the Governor's Mansion from the Illinois State Historical Society.

CHANGING
WITH
THE TIMES
1897–1968

John R. Tanner
Cora Edith English Tanner
(1897–1901)

John R. Tanner and his wife, Cora Edith English Tanner, began their life as governor and first lady in high style with the first official inaugural ball held in Illinois. In contrast with the less stately receptions hosted in the Governor's Mansion in years prior, this event took place in the Capitol building amid lavishly decorated rooms. During the grand march, the first lady carried a luxuriant bouquet of more than one thousand violets tied with purple velvet ribbons. This gesture hinted at the opulence she would bring to the remodeling and redecoration of the mansion during her husband's term. A Springfield socialite as well as a woman of letters who had studied abroad, she introduced cosmopolitan flair and sophistication to the residence's rooms and grounds.

In contrast to his wife, the daughter of a wealthy real estate businessman, Governor Tanner was the son of a farmer. After serving in the Civil War under General William T. Sherman, he returned to Illinois to farm before launching his political career with the Republican party in 1870. As governor, he refused to use the National Guard to break labor strikes. He also worked to end the importation of replacement workers and armed strikebreakers from outside Illinois. When the Spanish-American War broke out in 1898, Tanner immediately mustered troops, activating the Illinois National Guard and receiving its officers at the mansion. In May of that year, four thousand troops passed in review by the mansion while the first lady waved a flag from the porch. In addition to presiding over events at the mansion, the first lady was known in her own right as an outspoken proponent of Black American rights.

By the time the Tanners moved into the mansion in 1897, it was barely habitable. Despite past remediation efforts, stench and moisture rose from the ground, the roof leaked, the floors were sunken, and the woodwork was rotten. An article in the *Illinois State Journal* opined that "the arrangement of the rooms on the first floor is in poor taste, and public receptions can only be held with

discomfort when there is a large attendance." Despite these overwhelming challenges, Cora was described as displaying "admirable tact and grace in her ministrations of hospitality." While there was general agreement that urgent action was required, there was argument within the legislature about how much money to allocate and whether it might be better to tear the house down and build a new one. When noted Chicago architect Daniel Burnham was consulted about the matter, he favored the latter idea. Governor Tanner strongly disagreed, remarking that "there is a great deal of sentiment associated with the old mansion. During the past forty years the most distinguished and greatest men in Illinois have visited there and I hope will continue to do so. It belongs to the people, and they are always welcome and the mistress and myself will try to make it pleasant for all those who call."

To this end, Tanner requested from the legislature an appropriation of no less than 30,000 dollars for necessary improvements, a large sum at the time. In an 1897 issue of the *Illinois State Journal*, he was quoted as saying, "If you do not appropriate this sum . . . I would prefer that nothing be appropriated. I can move from there and reside at a hotel." Ultimately, the legislature appropriated the desired sum and plans for renovation and remodeling began. Springfield architect George H. Helmle, who launched his career

in Chicago after the great fire of 1871, was contracted to guide the project. Historical accounts indicate that the first lady played a significant role in the design. According to an 1898 article in the *Chicago Inter Ocean*, "The character of the house is due to her good taste and largely to her energy. She has been architect and construction 'boss,' as well as director of decorating and furnishing."

The exterior remodeling included two dramatic changes. The first was the reconfiguration of the entrance porch, originally approached by a single course of broad steps. The new design featured divided stairs ascending to the porch, beneath which a porte cochère and entrance opened to the ground floor to improve circulation at large-scale events. With the addition of rusticated stonework and a pressed-iron cornice, the original Greek Revival character of the porch was updated to late nineteenth-century style. Styles of the times also influenced a second and even more prominent alteration—the installation of a steep mansard roof that hid the original cupola. Significant changes were also made to the interior, particularly the replacement of the original elliptical staircase with a rectangular one with a carved balustrade and ornamental posts inspired by Château de Fontainebleau in France. On the second-floor landing, twelve columns finished in white and gold and mounted with electric lights illuminated the stair hall at night.

PREVIOUS PAGES In 1900, the sight of women driving by the mansion on Jackson Street was as much a sign of changing times as the mansion's newly remodeled mansard roof.

OPPOSITE Clockwise from upper left: Governors John R. Tanner, Charles S. Deneen, Frank O. Lowden, and Richard Yates Jr.

RIGHT A view of the mansion during the Tanner administration shows the new roof that concealed the cupola beneath a steep mansard.

On the ground floor, the service areas were reconfigured to meet the needs of large social functions, with a wide entrance hall opening from the porte cochère and flanked by men's and ladies' cloakrooms. Rooms originally designed for service functions were repurposed to include a governor's office and a billiards room enjoyed by male visitors and members of the press. Ornamental touches featuring colored tile floors, polished Tennessee marble wainscoting, and timbered ceilings completed the transformation. To accommodate some functions previously housed on the ground floor, the kitchen wing was enlarged. In 1899, a striking two-story carriage house and stable of pressed brick and stone was added to the grounds and fitted out with horse stalls and a carriage bay. As an equestrian, the first lady likely played an important role in its design.

With tapestry-covered walls and ceilings featuring designs of cherubs and vines amid delicate plaster appliqué, the interior redecoration demonstrated the first lady's European taste. Rooms ranging in palette from blue and pink to olive green and red featured weighty Empire-style mantels, mahogany wainscoting, and heavy dropped beams. A reporter from the *Illinois State Journal* remarked, "The rear parlor on the west shall have the most striking decorations in the suite. Rich Turkish red, relieved by gold stripes, will give its bold beauty to this room and will be a strong contrast to the delicate shades employed in the decorations on the opposite side of the hall." The decorations of the Family Dining Room revealed the influence of Old World European design with heavy ceiling timbers framing dark blue panels figured with a Dutch Renaissance motif.

Following the work's completion, the Tanners hosted a large public reception with state legislators as their guests. "Inasmuch as the change was made possible through the liberal appropriation voted by these legislators, they were interested in the result of the expenditure," reported the *Chicago Inter Ocean*. "The general verdict seemed to be that the money was well used. In place of a dingy and unsanitary pile, they saw a cheerful, well-arranged home in keeping with the conservative taste of the people of the state."

Richard Yates Jr.
Helen Wadsworth Yates
(1901–1905)

In 1901, Richard Yates Jr., son of Illinois governor Richard Yates, became the state's twenty-second governor. Having worked as a lawyer and a newspaperman for the *Jacksonville Daily Journal*, he entered public service in 1885, acting as a city attorney and a judge and running unsuccessfully as a United States representative before becoming the Republican gubernatorial nominee in 1900. A dark horse in the race, he was only forty years of age at the time of his election. For Yates Jr., taking residency in the Governor's Mansion meant a return to his childhood home, a place about which he had vivid recollections. The commencement of his adult time in the mansion was marked with an inaugural concert by the First

GEORGE H. HELMLE
Architect George H. Helmle (1853–1927) was the son of a German-born woodcarver, William, and his wife, Elise, a milliner, who arrived in Springfield in 1851. Helmle launched his career in Chicago in the aftermath of the great fire of 1871, then returned to his hometown to start what became Helmle & Helmle, Architects, a multi-generational architectural dynasty largely responsible for shaping the Springfield skyline. Among the designs the firm completed are the stone pavilion in Lincoln Park near Oak Ridge Cemetery, the Saint John's Hospital, and many homes for prominent Springfield residents. Helmle & Helmle also designed schools, churches, and part of the Sangamo Electric complex. The firm guided the renovation of the Governor's Mansion carried out by Governor Joseph W. Fifer and First Lady Gertrude Lewis Fifer in 1889, as well as its major remodeling during the Tanner administration. He later designed the Young Women's Christian Association building erected across the street from the mansion, since demolished. In his 1927 obituary, the *Illinois State Journal* wrote, "He thoroughly understood the architectural beauty and symmetry of building and many of the structures which were the results of his planning were nothing less than poems in mortar, brick and stone."

OPPOSITE In addition to dramatically altering the architectural features of the mansion, the Tanner administration's remodeling increased its size with a two-story service wing, where the heating system's boiler was relocated, as shown in floor plans depicting the circa 1900 wing.

FOLLOWING PAGES Although hidden from view outside the mansion, the buried cupola is still visible from within, where it can be seen through the oculus of the stair hall's domed ceiling.

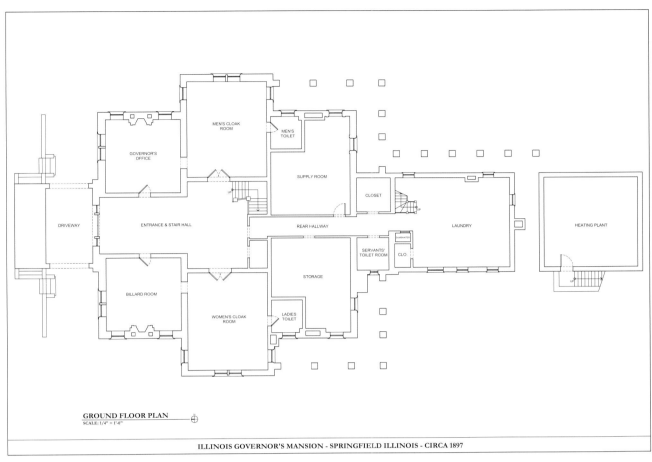

GROUND FLOOR PLAN
SCALE: 1/4" = 1'-0"

ILLINOIS GOVERNOR'S MANSION - SPRINGFIELD ILLINOIS - CIRCA 1897

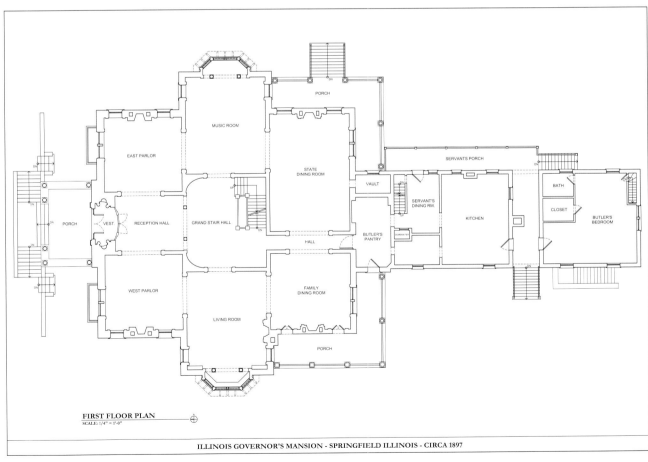

FIRST FLOOR PLAN
SCALE: 1/4" = 1'-0"

ILLINOIS GOVERNOR'S MANSION - SPRINGFIELD ILLINOIS - CIRCA 1897

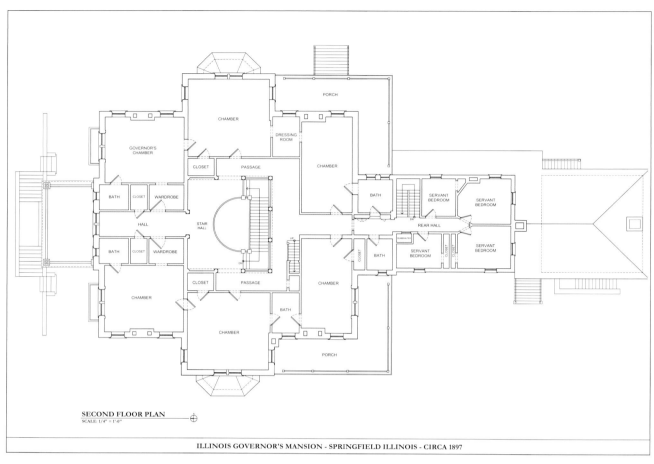

SECOND FLOOR PLAN
SCALE: 1/4" = 1'-0"

ILLINOIS GOVERNOR'S MANSION - SPRINGFIELD ILLINOIS - CIRCA 1897

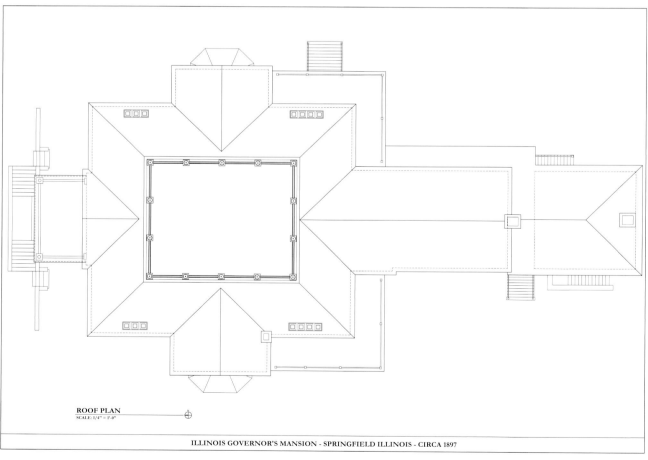

ROOF PLAN
SCALE: 1/4" = 1'-0"

ILLINOIS GOVERNOR'S MANSION - SPRINGFIELD ILLINOIS - CIRCA 1897

CORA EDITH ENGLISH TANNER

The daughter of a prosperous Springfield real estate businessman, Cora Edith English Tanner (1859–1946) came of age in the highest echelons of the city's social life. She began her education at Springfield High School and the Bettie Stuart Institute before traveling to the British Isles and Europe with family. While there, she continued her education, gaining sufficient fluency in German to become a skilled translator. Cora was likely introduced to her future husband, John R. Tanner, by his daughter, a former school friend. Tanner, a widower whose political career was rapidly advancing, was said to have been instantly enamored. It was related in the press that he proposed several times during their courtship, but Cora refused to accept his hand until he was elected governor. The couple wed on December 30, 1896, only twelve days before his inauguration. As first lady, she brought social élan and cosmopolitan flair to the mansion, supervising its redecoration and presiding over elegant gatherings. A keen supporter of human rights, Cora wrote a statement denouncing lynching and mob law in 1899 that was widely published. In it, she stated, "There is no fit time to ignore the law. Protection is the religion of our Nation, and the law protects, defends, and prescribes for all emergencies, not in the heat of passion, with inflamed, hysterical brain and barbarous thirst for blood, but scruple for scruple and dram for dram, carefully weighing our offenses, no matter how hideous the crime or how petty the sin. We cannot live in this world without justice, nor in the world to come without mercy."

OPPOSITE Springfield architect John I. Rinaker Jr., a member of the Illinois Society of Architects, drew plans for many prominent projects in the city including the Masonic Temple, Odd Fellows Hall, and other business and residential structures.

· SOUTH · ELEVATION ·

· STABLE ·
· FOR · THE ·
GOVERNOR'S · MANSION
· SPRINGFIELD ·

SCALE : ¼ IN. = ONE · FOOT ·

· OFFICE · OF · THE · SUPERVISING · ARCHITECT ·
· STATE · OF · ILLINOIS ·
· R · BRUCE · WATSON · ⑥
· CHICAGO ·
JOHN · I · RINAKER · ASSOCIATE · ARCHITECT · SPRINGFIELD ·

CARRIAGE HOUSE AND STABLE

The carriage house and stable that Springfield architect John I. Rinaker Jr. (1865–1939) created for the Governor's Mansion in 1899 expressed the eclecticism in vogue at the time. An enthusiastic equestrian, First Lady Cora Tanner likely collaborated closely with Rinaker in its design. English in inspiration, the building combined Georgian elements, including the entrance's articulated stone masonry surround, heavy stone quoins on the corners, and spherical pinnacles. The low-sweeping slate roof, chimney cap, and leaded glass windows introduced Elizabethan character. Pressed red brick, a decorative element popular in late nineteenth-century American architecture, added more ornamental detail. Taken together, these elements resulted in a building that was both handsome and romantic. The structure was demolished and replaced in the 1970s during the Richard B. Ogilvie administration and converted into a garage and staff quarters more closely resembling the restored mansion and new addition.

Regiment Illinois National Guard band on the grounds, followed by a reception for the general public attended by an estimated two thousand citizens.

Bipartisanship was a theme throughout the residency of Yates Jr. and his wife, Helen Wadsworth Yates. Following the inauguration, First Lady Yates issued a handwritten note to every senator and representative, inviting them to the mansion on Wednesday evenings. She told a reporter that she "desires the members of the legislature to regard the executive mansion as their social rendezvous during the session, and is anxious to have them feel at home there." The governor made it known that all Democratic legislators were specifically invited to these receptions. During these events, political divisions were dropped and "Democrats and Republicans alike partook of the good cheer and fellowship." The general public was also invited into the life of the mansion, according to an account in the *Chicago Daily Tribune* reporting the first lady's wish that "the rooms on the first floor should be shown to any persons desiring to look over the mansion."

During his campaign, Yates claimed no agenda or causes of his own, allowing legislation to come from the General Assembly. Among the bills Yates signed was a law limiting child labor—the first of its kind in any state. The first lady, an advocate for social reform, hosted reformer Jane Addams, founder of the Hull House settlement house, at the mansion. During her visit, Addams spoke about her work on behalf of working-class immigrants in Chicago. Other distinguished visitors included Abraham Lincoln's son Robert Todd Lincoln, who came to inspect the newly reconstructed tomb at his father's grave at Oak Ridge Cemetery in 1901. Vice President Theodore Roosevelt also stopped at the mansion that year and returned again as president in 1903. Musical events were often staged on the grounds, including a concert by the band of the Eighth Infantry Regiment, a Black-American unit of the then-segregated Illinois National Guard. An article in the *Illinois State Register* observed that the scene would have made Booker T. Washington's "heart leap with joy and many inspirations would have been furnished his mind as to the rights of his race."

Yates Jr. contracted typhoid fever in 1902, and the mansion's persistent sewage problems may have been the cause. Early the next year, the mansion's boiler failed, leaving the building heated only by scattered coal grates, prompting the legislature to pass a

LEFT First Lady Helen Wadsworth Yates was known for dressing the house on special occasions with a "bewildering confusion" of decorations, as seen here in preparation for President Theodore Roosevelt's 1903 visit. Japanese lanterns festooned with greenery and Roosevelt's name emblazoned on the fireplace enliven the dining room's decor.

ABRAHAM LINCOLN TOMB

On April 24, 1865, less than two weeks after Lincoln died, a group of Springfield citizens formed the National Lincoln Monument Association to raise funds to erect a suitable memorial in Springfield. Four years later, construction of the memorial, designed by noted American neoclassical sculptor Larkin Goldsmith Mead, began. The tomb he created features an obelisk atop a square base housing an oval receiving room and a burial chamber. In addition to conceiving the architecture of the structure, Mead designed bronze sculptures, including a statue of Lincoln and representations of the infantry, navy, artillery, and cavalry. By the time the State of Illinois acquired the monument in 1895, it had fallen into disrepair and a program of rebuilding was launched. When the work was finished in 1901, Lincoln's son Robert Todd Lincoln visited the tomb to inspect the work. At his request, his father's remains were moved to their final resting place, a concrete-filled crypt located beneath the floor of the burial chamber where they would be safe from disturbance. From 1930 to 1931, another project renovated the interior, creating the spaces as they are now.

RIGHT An 1869 certificate issued to those who contributed fifty cents to the building of the monument.

OPPOSITE One of a pair of hand-painted vases displayed in the East Parlor belonged to John T. Stuart, a friend and former law partner of Abraham Lincoln, and was given to the mansion by his granddaughter.

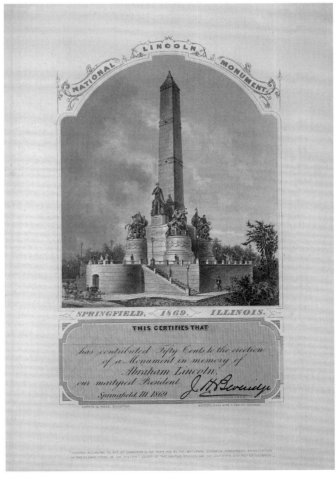

modest appropriation for repairs and refurbishment. The first lady supervised minor redecoration projects, the most significant one being replacing the original floors with new oak ones. Former First Lady Tanner's tapestry wallcoverings were removed, and several rooms were repainted in new colors. One of First Lady Yates's most imaginative changes occurred in the front parlors, where she replaced mantelpieces with large mirrors, "giving the appearance to the rooms of extending indefinitely into space."

Charles S. Deneen
Bina Day Maloney Deneen
(1905–1913)

In 1904, Republican Charles S. Deneen was elected as the state's chief executive. Previously a member of the Illinois House of Representatives, Deneen would go on after his two terms as governor to become a United States senator. A supporter of the rights of Black Americans throughout his career, Deneen endorsed the passage of an anti-lynching law in his first year as governor. The law responded to an increase in racial violence in Illinois towns and cities and those of other American states. Not long afterward, in 1909, Illinois saw one of its most infamous instances of lynching when a mob numbering in the thousands gathered to witness the hanging of William James, a Black resident of Cairo accused of a heinous murder. Mob violence had visited Springfield the previous year, with three days of havoc targeting Black citizens in what became known as the Springfield race riot. Deneen monitored the event from the State House and eventually succeeded in quelling it by calling up the National Guard.

During his administration, Deneen signed several appropriations of funds for mansion repairs, but conditions continued to be unstable, as demonstrated by a large chunk of plaster falling on his pillow. First Lady Bina Day Maloney Deneen made few changes to the mansion other than directing the work of painters who repainted the exterior yellow in 1909 and putty gray in 1912, as well as painting the rooms within. By this time, Deneen was using the mansion as his primary place of work and official seat. In these rooms, the Deneens received many guests, including President William Taft, who visited in 1911 while speaking before the Illinois General Assembly, and former president Theodore Roosevelt in 1912. According to a newspaper report, politics were not discussed during Roosevelt's visit to the Republican governor's home. Instead, stories of Abraham Lincoln abounded, recounted by influential Illinois financier and industrialist John W. Bunn, who was a personal friend of Lincoln.

Although the first lady was described as demure and unassuming, she pursued a variety of social and women's rights initiatives during her time in the mansion. In 1907, she opened a boys' club room on the ground floor as the headquarters of the Springfield anti-cigarette movement. "Boys who have 'the habit' and need help to get free" were offered help and encouragement "any day between four and five o'clock." She also demonstrated her support

PORTRAIT OF PATRICK HENRY

In 1909, Governor Charles S. Deneen signed legislation appropriating one thousand dollars for a portrait to be painted by renowned Chicago artist Ralph E. Clarkson (1861–1942) of eighteenth-century Virginia governor Patrick Henry. Henry, who commissioned an expedition to secure the lands bounded by the Great Lakes and the Ohio and Mississippi Rivers—of which Illinois was a component—is considered by some to have been the first governor of Illinois. Depicted in a red overcoat, with glasses propped upon his head and a letter held in an expressively rendered hand, Henry sets his gaze to the distance as if, perhaps, looking toward the western lands. Although the painting is a close likeness to one painted by American portraitist Thomas Sully in 1815, Clarkson contributed additional details that enliven the composition. These details and the artist's dramatic brushwork bring power and animation to the portrait. Henry's granddaughter believed that the painting combined Henry's strength of character with "other gentler traits" and "was especially happy in the rendering of a hand peculiarly characteristic of her grandfather." The completed portrait was displayed in the State House for many years, before being moved to the West Parlor of the mansion, where it hung when President Franklin D. Roosevelt met with Governor Henry Horner there in 1936.

SPRINGFIELD RACE RIOT

The Springfield race riot erupted in August 1908. A large mob of White Americans and European immigrants committed mass racial violence targeting Springfield's Black population. The event was spurred by allegations of rape and murder against two Black men, one of whom was eventually tried, convicted, and hanged, while the other was freed after his accuser recanted. As rioting persisted for three days, both Black and White residents were killed, dozens of homes and businesses were destroyed, and devastating property damage was suffered, overwhelmingly by Black citizens. The fact that the violence, described as "a proxy for the story of race in America," occurred in the hometown of Abraham Lincoln shocked many Americans. Rioters lynched the elderly William Donnegan (right) across the street from his home, on the corner of Spring and Edwards Streets, on land which today is part of the State Capitol Complex. The onetime conductor on the Underground Railroad had played an active role in the city's Black community during the Civil War era. As a cobbler, he is remembered for making shoes for Lincoln. The riot catalyzed the formation of the National Association for the Advancement of Colored People in 1909. Illinois artist Preston Jackson was commissioned by the NAACP in 2008 to create a memorial to commemorate the riot. His inspiration for the sculpture, *Acts of Intolerance,* came from an old photograph of two charred chimneys rising from the smoldering rubble of burned-out buildings.

ABOVE Springfield residents struggled to contain the vandalism and fires that caused the destruction of many homes and businesses, primarily owned by Black citizens, during the Springfield race riot.

CLARENCE LIGGINS

Clarence Liggins (1878–1975) worked for several Illinois secretaries of state and governors in a variety of capacities ranging from cook to chauffeur. At the time of Governor Henry Horner's death in 1940, he dressed the remains and accompanied the body from Winnetka to Chicago for burial. During the Springfield race riot of 1908, reportedly at the bidding of Illinois Secretary of State James A. Rose, he proceeded to the Governor's Mansion to seek sanctuary and protect the house while Governor Charles S. Deneen was in the State House. In 1974, he recalled telling the secretary "not to worry about it, that I'd be there when she went down in ashes. And I got my rifle and even my walking cane that shot a bullet." He and some family members took refuge in the mansion for three days, staying well away from the windows to prevent the soldiers and members of the mob from seeing them.

BINA DAY MALONEY DENEEN

Although she described herself as a "home woman," Bina Day Maloney Deneen (1868–1950) began adult life as a career woman, teaching and working as a stenographer and typist while living in a Chicago boarding house. In 1891, she married law student and future governor of Illinois Charles S. Deneen. While fulfilling her role as first lady by presiding over state and civic events, Bina extended her interests well beyond the mansion's walls. Past president of the Englewood Woman's Club, formed to promote the humanities, and member of the Chicago Woman's Club, she was a longtime advocate of the woman's club movement. She welcomed suffragists into the Governor's Mansion, hosting a reception for the Illinois Equal Suffrage Association in 1911. The next year, she entertained delegates of the group who had returned to Springfield, accompanied by two hundred suffragists, to lobby for passage of an equal suffrage law. Jane Addams was among the guests. An active supporter of the Young Women's Christian Association, the first lady hosted several meetings at the mansion to plan fundraising efforts to construct a Springfield home for the organization. In 1912, she helped lay the cornerstone of the new building (above), a handsome structure designed by architect George H. Helmle that stood across the street from the mansion until it was demolished in 2017.

LEFT This photograph captures the serene elegance of the Music Parlor in 1905 before First Lady Florence Pullman Lowden did an extensive renovation in 1917.

151

for women's suffrage and the Young Women's Christian Association. A devout Christian, the first lady hosted prayer meetings led by professional baseball player turned evangelist Billy Sunday and study meetings of the Via Christi group, co-sponsored by her friend Catharine Frazee Lindsay, poet Vachel Lindsay's mother.

Frank O. Lowden
Florence Pullman Lowden
(1917–1921)

Frank O. Lowden's story of political success is a classic American tale of determination and ingenuity. Raised in poverty on an Iowa farm, Lowden taught in a one-room schoolhouse for five years before being admitted to the University of Iowa. After graduating, he took courses in stenography, hoping the practical skill would win him a place at a Chicago law firm. The strategy succeeded, and soon Lowden was spending days working in law offices while taking night courses at the Union College of Law, from which he graduated as valedictorian. After gradually ascending the ranks of the Republican party, he won a seat in the United States House of Representatives in 1906. He served two terms before becoming Illinois's governor in 1917. Lowden came to the governorship in troubling times. World War I was in its third year and Germany's aggressions increased the likelihood of America's involvement. On April 2, 1917—just three months into Lowden's term—President Woodrow Wilson called for a declaration of war against Germany and Austria-Hungary, plunging the nation into the European conflict.

Closer to home, racial tension erupted with the 1919 Chicago race riot, when groups of White people attacked Black citizens over a period of eight days, leaving thirty-eight people—twenty-three of them Black—dead and more than 500 injured. Between one and two thousand people, most of them Black, lost their homes. It was the worst of many riots and disturbances during what was called the "Red Summer" of 1919, which saw widespread race riots and White supremacist terrorism. Lowden's handling of the riot earned him wide respect.

The governor was joined in the mansion by his wife, Florence Pullman Lowden, the daughter of wealthy industrialist George M. Pullman, manufacturer of the Pullman sleeping cars. By the time the couple moved into the mansion in 1917, repairs were drastically required. Although the 30,000 dollars appropriated for refurbishment during the Tanner administration was a sizeable sum, it

LEFT In 1919, King Albert and Queen Elisabeth of Belgium (center left), accompanied by their son Prince Leopold (far left), toured America, including a visit to Springfield. They are pictured here at the Lincoln Tomb beside Governor Frank Lowden (center right) and First Lady Florence Lowden (behind the queen).

OSSIAN COLE SIMONDS

In the late 1900s and early twentieth century, landscape gardener Ossian Cole Simonds (1855–1931) gained fame as a pioneer of the Prairie Style movement, which celebrated the horizontal lines of the Midwestern landscape and the use of native plants. In 1917, First Lady Florence Pullman Lowden chose Simonds to re-envision the grounds of the Governor's Mansion, relaxing its formality and imparting an inviting character. To this end, Simonds softened the severe lines of the architecture with awnings and containers filled with grasses and trailing greenery. Rather than manicured, geometric plantings, the garden beds he designed were naturalistic compositions of shrubbery and flowers. The recipient of awards from the Exposition Universelle in Paris and the Architectural League of New York, Simonds also founded the American Society of Landscape Architects in 1899 and published *Landscape Gardening*, a widely consulted book that advocated seeking inspiration from nature. Celebrated for cemetery designs, including a portion of Chicago's Graceland Cemetery and Arboretum, Simonds also completed notable projects such as Chicago's Lincoln Park, Morton Arboretum, and Fort Sheridan Army Post, as well as buildings for the state universities of Iowa and Maryland.

ABOVE Awnings were added to the exterior of the mansion during the Lowden administration.

OPPOSITE A cast-iron fountain that was moved from the State Capitol to the mansion in 1887 has been used over time to water horses and hold decorative plantings of flowers. Now it serves as a water feature in the East Garden.

was inadequate to address persistent problems to modernize the house at this time. Arguing for a new appropriation, the governor remarked to a reporter that "the heating apparatus, the plumbing, the electric light wiring were all antiquated and dangerous. The foundations of the building itself in places needed strengthening." With two decades having elapsed since the last redecoration, there was also general consensus that the decor needed to be improved.

In 1917, the state approved 26,000 dollars for modernizing the mansion's systems, but the sum fell far short of what was needed. At that point, the first lady stepped in, offering to pay for some of the improvements from her own funds. Speaking with a reporter, the governor discussed the situation, saying, "Mrs. Lowden asked me if there was any objection to her using her own money to supply the deficiency. I told her there was none, if her patriotism was equal to it. . . . The upshot of it was that she expended $25,000 of her own money in addition to the appropriation in permanent reconstruction of the Mansion."

A portion of funds went toward updating the interior design, with the first lady subduing the earlier bold color palette and softening what she perceived as stiff formality. A reporter for the *Illinois State Journal* who toured the mansion in late 1917 commented, "It had not been her intention to have anything made elaborate or impressive, merely to put the house in good order, making it harmonious and dignified." The reporter observed that the selection of furniture was "in line with the prevailing idea of economy and conservation" in deference to wartime financial restraint. In addition to purchasing new objects for the mansion, the first lady also brought a number of furnishings and artworks from the Lowdens' private home.

In the first lady's redecoration, the strong hues of the receiving rooms were replaced with cream tones, with furnishings and drapery providing color. The Northeast Parlor, previously decorated in vying shades of pink that had prompted one reporter to call it "the War of the Roses," was decorated with newly upholstered furniture that matched the original pink velvet curtains. In the adjoining Music Parlor, green draperies offered contrast to cream-colored walls and mahogany wainscoting. "The room is a quiet and harmonious setting for the thing for which it was designed, music," wrote an approving reporter from the *Illinois State Journal*. The dining room also received a makeover in shades of cream and green, replacing former First Lady Tanner's bold palette of red, blue, black, and gold.

First Lady Lowden expressed the intention of imparting a home-like atmosphere to the mansion, as seen in the parlor adjoining the dining room, which she decorated with family pictures and paintings, a deep couch, and inviting chairs. The same reporter wrote, "It is a room in which . . . one might sit down a moment before the fire and feel at home." Changes to the grounds, directed by well-known landscape gardener Ossian Cole Simonds, also indicated the mansion's new air of approachability. "The old, law-abiding yellow stone coping, surmounted with terrifying iron pickets, which used to surround the yard, is no more," one reporter

FLORENCE PULLMAN LOWDEN

Florence Pullman Lowden (1868–1937) was the daughter of wealthy railroad-car manufacturer George Pullman. According to the 1896 wedding announcement in *The New York Times*, she received multiple proposals of marriage from titled European aristocrats before accepting the hand of lawyer Frank O. Lowden, son of an Iowa farmer and future governor of Illinois. The article speculated that it was "the serious quality" in her character that drew the two together. By the time of her marriage, she had already developed a keen interest in Jane Addams's settlement work, as well as projects aimed at improving popular access to art. As first lady, she promoted women's suffrage and the care of victims of polio, which afflicted two of her daughters. She supervised and partially funded the redecoration and landscaping of the mansion. During World War I, she hosted the Illinois Women's Division of the Council of National Defense and frequented the local Red Cross shop, where she and one of her daughters sewed garments for soldiers from Illinois. She also supported the war effort by encouraging Illinoisians to purchase Liberty Bonds.

observed. Awnings and flowerboxes relaxed the appearance of the entrance porch and naturalistic plantings softened the grounds.

Upon completing the project, the first lady hosted an at-home event attended by seventy-five women. In keeping with wartime food conservation efforts, she served "cakes and war candies. . . . None of the dainty little cakes were made with wheat flour, and the candies were all made with molasses and syrups and brown sugar, instead of the white granulated sugar, which the government is shipping to France." Festivities at the mansion continued that year with a rehearsal of an Illinois centennial pageant on the newly landscaped grounds.

To honor the centennial, former president Theodore Roosevelt and his wife visited Springfield and stayed in the newly refurbished mansion. "This has been a day of great activity!" wrote First Lady Lowden in her journal. "Roosevelts being here has made the house a Mecca for politicians, many of whom are here for the Centennial." Demonstrating the mansion's new air of approach-ability, a twelve-year-old boy rode his bicycle to the house and rang the doorbell, hoping to see the former president. The governor's daughter Florence Lowden greeted him at the door. Soon afterward, Roosevelt descended the stairs and took the boy's hand, saying, "Young America first. I have had plenty of men call upon me, Lawrence, but you are the first boy to call upon me."

Henry Horner
(1933–1940)

Elected during the depths of the Great Depression, progressive Democrat Henry Horner became Illinois's first Jewish governor. Navigating the tough political and economic landscape of the time with great integrity and a commitment to fiscal responsibility, he showed empathy toward those in need. Among his important initiatives was a bill establishing the state's first permanent sales tax in order raise much-needed revenue.

JANE ADDAMS

Jane Addams (1860–1935), a political activist and daughter of one of Abraham Lincoln's admirers and supporters, John H. Addams, won worldwide recognition in the early twentieth century for her pioneering social work and support of women's rights. During a tour of Europe from 1887 to 1888, she visited Toynbee Hall in London's East End, considered the world's first settlement house. In 1889, she and her colleague, Ellen G. Starr, leased a large home in Chicago with the goal of creating a similar establishment. This became Hull House, a center for civic and social life, educational and philanthropic enterprises, and improvement of conditions in Chicago's industrial neighborhoods. Within two years, Hull House was host to two thousand people a week—most of them recently arrived European immigrants—with kindergarten classes in the morning and courses in the evening in what became virtually a night school. By 1911, Hull House had expanded to encompass thirteen buildings. As its reputation grew, Addams became an internationally recognized speaker on subjects ranging from civic responsibility to racial equality and women's rights. A suffragist, Addams espoused the view that women should not only have the right to vote but should also possess the power to realize their aspirations. Cofounder of the American Civil Liberties Union in 1920, she was the first woman to receive an honorary degree from Yale University and was awarded the Nobel Peace Prize in 1931. This 1892 portrait from the Jane Addams-Hull House Museum was painted by Alice Kellogg Tyler (1862–1900).

ABOVE Artist Floyd Brackney (1887–1943) painted a sensitive portrait of Governor Henry Horner that marries the historic convention of red drapery in the upper left corner with a modern treatment of the subject and his clothing. The portrait captures the kind countenance of the governor, who was known for compassionate social reform.

RIGHT President Franklin D. Roosevelt greeted by an enthusiastic crowd in front of the mansion in 1936. He visited Springfield during a tour of Midwestern states to inspect drought conditions and explore assistance to farmers.

HENRY HORNER LINCOLN COLLECTION

Governor Henry Horner's passion for collecting published books, pamphlets, and prints relating to Abraham Lincoln began in 1900, when he worked as law partner to the son of the former president's friend and colleague Henry C. Whitney. The office's library included books that Lincoln had used. "I started practice holding [them], and the atmosphere thus created had a powerful effect upon me," he told a reporter. Throughout the remainder of his life, he acquired rare books and pamphlets related to the former president. While governor, he housed the collection in a second-floor bedroom of the mansion. The weight was so great that a truss was installed in the attic and the bookcases were suspended from it. A keen supporter of the Illinois State Historical Library, Horner appropriated funds to support its mission and promote the purchase of Lincoln documents in the midst of the Depression. The governor bequeathed his collection to the library in 1940, stipulating that "you make it henceforth permanently available to any and all who may come to study Lincoln. If you can do this you will make me the happiest of men." The material formed the foundation of what is now the Abraham Lincoln Presidential Library and Museum.

State taxes on real estate and personal property were also initiated in an effort to support the state's faltering economy and aid the indigent. Horner's fiscal policies were unpopular among many, but his support of the Twenty-First Amendment, which repealed Prohibition, during his first year in office had widespread appeal.

Horner was interested in reform on a variety of fronts, including elections. During his tenure, a permanent voter registration system was enacted that required voters' signatures to match records maintained by election officials. Workers' rights and unionization were also of pressing concern, with the governor inviting representatives of the unions and mine owners, as well as community mayors, to meet at the mansion on several occasions. Intolerant of graft and patronage appointments that fattened state payrolls, Horner drew the ire of Chicago Mayor Edward Kelly and Patrick Nash, leaders of the Cook County Democratic organization known as the Kelly-Nash Machine. During these times of fraught political relations, Horner met at the mansion with inter-party opponents. He also received President Franklin D. Roosevelt, who came to Springfield to address challenges caused by a large-scale drought.

Horner not only made lasting changes to Illinois's social and fiscal landscape; he also made a significant contribution to memorializing Abraham Lincoln's legacy by amassing a large collection of Lincoln-related printed material that he left to the state. As a member of the Lincoln Memorial Commission, he considered how best to commemorate the late president in Illinois. Rather than erecting a monument, as some suggested, the commission successfully advocated for the development of a state-owned system of sites at places that had played a role in Lincoln's life. These included New Salem, where Lincoln lived from 1831 to 1837, the Vandalia State House, and the Mount Pulaski Courthouse, all of which are open to the public today. As Horner struggled with ill health near the end of his second term, he bequeathed his highly regarded collection of Lincolniana to the Illinois State Historical Library to ensure that the materials he had amassed over a period of four decades would be available to anyone interested in the subject.

Dwight H. Green
Mabel Kingston Green
(1941–1949)

Spurred by a backlash against the New Deal and the Democratic party that shaped it, Republican candidate Dwight H. Green won the Illinois governorship in 1940. He had previously served as the special assistant to the U.S. attorney for the Northern District of Illinois, where his primary responsibility was fighting organized crime operations, including Al Capone's Chicago gang. During his first year as governor, the Japanese bombed Pearl Harbor, thrusting the country, and Illinois, into World War II. Throughout his first term as governor, Green played an active role in marshaling the state's war effort and building civilian support. During his second term as governor, he was required to meet

many postwar challenges, including the acute shortage of housing for returning veterans.

As many Illinois governors had discovered, the residence provided by the state was sorely inadequate to meet the demands it was intended to fulfill. A newspaper account from 1941 describes it as "badly in need of repair, so much so [that] legislators suggested this year that it be torn down and a new one constructed." Indeed, a commission appointed by the legislators considered a bill appropriating 100,000 dollars to build a new executive mansion. Among many serious issues was the concern that the floors were in danger of collapse whenever a large crowd assembled. Due to fiscal concerns, however, the governor advocated for a smaller appropriation—which was approved—of fifty thousand dollars for repair, replacement of equipment, and redecoration.

State architect C. Herrick Hammond oversaw structural changes to the mansion, while First Lady Mabel Kingston Green supervised modest updates to the interior design, much needed after the effects of Depression-era economizing and Governor Horner's bachelor living. Her work ranged from freshening the decor of many rooms with "charming new appointments and decoration" to improving the family bedrooms and bathrooms. The first lady also addressed smaller yet pressing concerns, including a shortage of linens, china, and tableware, depleted by constant use and the passage of time. According to a 1941 account, "Mrs. Green found there was hardly enough dishes, including plates, glasses, platters, to serve, to say nothing of a shortage of silverware."

Following the Pearl Harbor bombing, Green addressed the people by radio from his office in the mansion, calling all Illinoisians to take part in defending the nation. Three days later, he gathered legislative leaders and state department heads at the mansion to discuss an appropriation request of sixteen million dollars for military activity. Even though a sense of wartime urgency prevailed at the house, the governor and first lady upheld the community tradition of hosting a Christmas reception on the grounds for children. A thirty-foot tree illuminated with three hundred lights was erected for the occasion. They also held a muted New Year's Day reception, offering hundreds of callers their first opportunity to see the mansion's improvements. According to an account in the *Illinois State Journal*, "Those who came to see what the mansion looked like after the renovation left well pleased. The interior of the old building is beautiful and is furnished in excellent taste." Later that year, actress Marlene Dietrich, while in Springfield for a war-bond rally, was among the high-profile wartime visitors to be entertained at the newly refurbished mansion.

From the beginning of America's involvement in World War II, Green, like President Roosevelt, embraced radio as a potent tool to inform the public of important events and to rally their support. In February of 1943, he made the first of a series of last-Sunday-of-the-month radio addresses to Illinois residents from the mansion, reporting on the state war effort and the welfare of Illinois service personnel. When the governor broadcast his second annual *Christmas from the Governor's Mansion* program over the WCBS channel, the first lady spoke to the women of Illinois. Throughout his administration, the governor routinely held in-person meetings of local and national importance at the mansion, including a dinner for Vice President Henry Wallace, a meeting with Chicago mayor and

PREVIOUS PAGES First Lady Mabel Green poses for a photograph in her office in the Southwest Sunroom in 1942. The room was located on the second story of a porch originally open to the air that was reconstructed and enclosed during the Emmerson administration (1929–1933).

RIGHT Governor and First Lady Green and their daughters step out in style from the rusticated stone portico of the mansion.

OPPOSITE With the simple silhouettes of its furnishings, long-pile carpet, and muted palette, the East Parlor expresses the 1940s aesthetic in fashion during the Green's residence.

Democratic state party chair Edward Kelly, and a 1946 luncheon during which legislators and scientists discussed the atomic bomb.

The first lady participated actively both in wartime efforts, such as gatherings of the Girl Scouts and USO parties at the mansion, as well as Republican party functions, such as a tea for a Colored Republican Women's Club, to which "all Republican women" were invited. Whether donating to blood banks or posing with fighter planes for newspaper photographs, she became the face of the administration's efforts to galvanize and recognize Illinois women's support during the war.

Adlai E. Stevenson II
Ellen Borden Stevenson (divorced 1949)
(1949–1953)

In 1948, Adlai E. Stevenson II, member of a prominent Illinois political family, was elected governor. With characteristic wit, he referred to his family's deep history in government by declaring that he had "a bad case of hereditary politics." A popular public speaker, Stevenson was in office for only one term but during that time left his mark on Illinois politics by further cracking down

ABOVE Governor Stevenson maintained an office on the ground floor of the mansion from which he wrote his concession speech after losing the 1952 presidential election.

OPPOSITE Despite his reputation as an intellectual, the Princeton-educated presidential candidate positioned himself as a man of the people with strong Midwestern values.

for President **ADLAI E. STEVENSON**

the man America needs

U.S.S. *ILLINOIS* SILVER SERVICE

During World War II, the United States Navy announced that it was planning to name one of its new battleships the U.S.S. *Illinois*. There had long been a tradition that a state for which a battleship was named would supply a complete silver service for the vessel. Thus, in April 1943, a delegation of Illinois naval veterans proposed that the Illinois General Assembly appropriate 20,000 dollars for a sterling-silver service for use in the officers' mess on the new *Illinois*. Most of the cost was funded by private donations. C. D. Peacock, one of Chicago's foremost retail jewelers, agreed to furnish the 359-piece set, which was fabricated by Watson Company in Attleboro, Massachusetts. The set includes large and small holloware pieces, such as punchbowls, tea and coffee services, and serving pieces embellished with seals of the U.S. Navy and the State of Illinois and decorated with the Illinois state flower, the violet. In addition, the collection included flatware, candelabras, and goblets with dolphin stems. It was estimated that four thousand ounces of silver were required to produce the set. The battleship for which it was designed was only one-quarter completed when Japan surrendered in 1945, but by that time the silver service was finished. In 1949, representatives from the U.S.S. *Illinois* legislative commission formally presented the service to Governor Adlai E. Stevenson II for use in the Illinois Governor's Mansion.

on corruption and working for constitutional reform. The entire nation took notice, and Stevenson became the Democratic nominee for United States president in 1952. As governor, he focused much of his energy on reform, targeting corruption in state government, deterring illegal gambling, reforming the state police, and introducing crime bills.

Stevenson's term coincided with a national trend known as the Second Red Scare. In step with Joseph McCarthy and others, the Illinois state legislature passed a bill outlawing membership in subversive groups and requiring public employees and candidates to sign a loyalty oath. Stevenson vetoed the bill, saying, "The whole notion of loyalty inquisitions is a natural characteristic of the police state, not of democracy. . . . I must, in good conscience, protest against any unnecessary suppression of our ancient rights as free men." During his time in office, he pursued agendas that positively affected the everyday lives of Illinoisians, including improving state highways and delivering aid to cities.

When Stevenson's marriage to Ellen Borden Stevenson ended in the first year of his term, his sister, Elizabeth "Buffy" Ives, became the acting first lady. Among the notable guests she helped her brother entertain were comedian Bob Hope, who came to Springfield to perform at the state fair, and United States Senator Hubert Humphrey. When Republican presidential candidate Dwight D. Eisenhower made a stop to visit the Lincoln Tomb in 1952, he declined an invitation to lunch at the official home of his political opponent. Ranging from a reception for eighth-grade Chicago students to annual luncheons for veterans, mansion events demonstrated the governor's commitment to all constituents. When the traditional New Year's Day reception was held in 1950, no invitations were issued "as the call is general." One thousand people attended.

According to Stevenson's sister, the governor found solace in the mansion during turbulent times. She recalled, "He loved the House—would take pride in walking through the lovely rooms and talk about the past when visitors came. From the beginning of warm weather to frost he ate breakfast on the porch outside the State Dining Room—also lunch when possible and always dinner in the garden." Although Stevenson resisted suggestions of redecorating the interior, he took a keen interest in the gardens and personally chose trees to replace twenty-nine elms that succumbed to blight. The one mansion improvement he did call for was the creation of a permanent library, which he named the Lloyd Lewis Library after a prominent Chicago historian and author. Stevenson also worked to secure historical artifacts, including Lincolniana, for the Illinois State Historical Society.

LEFT The State Dining Room, pictured here in 1952 during the Stevenson administration, featured flowered wallcoverings and chairs upholstered in damask woven with the seal of Illinois.

By spring of 1952, Governor Stevenson was talked about enthusiastically as a prospective Democratic nominee for president. Returning to Springfield from the Democratic National Convention in Chicago where he had won the nomination, he was greeted by a crowd estimated at twenty-five thousand people. Following the nomination, President Truman sent a longhand note delivered by messenger that read, in part, "If it is worth anything to you, you have my wholehearted support and cooperation." As Stevenson grappled with the strong emotions these events stirred, he sought a way to calm his feelings and direct his thoughts. That evening, he made arrangements with the caretaker of Abraham Lincoln's former Springfield home to visit it. Slipping out of the mansion late at night, he walked to the house, where he sat in Lincoln's rocking chair for an hour. "Beyond admitting to a few friends years later that the incident occurred," wrote Stevenson's biographer Porter McKeever, "he never discussed why he did it or what he felt other than to say that on the walk back to the mansion on the dark street he felt a deep calm about the task that lay before him."

Following Stevenson's nomination, the chaos of starting a campaign fewer than one hundred days before the election, with no funds nor organization in place, was intense. An office was set up near the mansion, but it filled quickly, and staffers moved into the house as well, even though it was never intended to be the campaign headquarters. Phone lines were so busy that the Democratic National Committee in Washington put in a separate switchboard for calls to the mansion. On election night, Stevenson sat in his mansion office, listening to the early returns broadcast by radio that foretold his defeat by Eisenhower. Later that night, he delivered a concession speech in which he pledged to continue working toward a time when "all God's children shall grow in freedom and dignity in a world at peace." When asked how he felt about his defeat, he said he "was reminded of a story that a fellow townsman of ours used to tell—Abraham Lincoln. They asked him how he felt once after an unsuccessful election. He said he felt like a little boy who had stubbed his toe in the dark. He said that he was too old to cry and it hurt too much to laugh."

William G. Stratton
Shirley Breckenridge Stratton
(1953–1961)

William G. Stratton became Illinois governor in 1953, during a time of optimism, patriotism, and post-World War II prosperity. With the rise of the middle class, modern household appliances, including televisions, were becoming prevalent in American homes. Large staffs of servants were no longer required, and in many households formality was relaxed. The Governor's Mansion was no exception to these trends. In 1955, Stratton told a reporter that he and First Lady Shirley Breckenridge Stratton "think the mansion ought to have a warm, homelike atmosphere in which our friends and the public

will feel welcome." To that end, the first lady guided a comprehensive redecoration of the house and the governor moved staff offices out of the mansion's ground floor to the State House, explaining, "It makes the executive mansion seem more like a home."

Before becoming governor, Stratton served the nation in a variety of capacities, as a two-term member of the United States House of Representatives, twice as Illinois state treasurer, and as a lieutenant in the United States Navy. During his time as governor, state hospital reforms were instituted to include more beds for patients, an improved state sales tax was initiated to fund schools, the first woman and the first Black American were appointed to cabinet level positions, and a bond issue was approved that funded the state's expressway system. Stratton considered the construction of the first two hundred miles of the Illinois tollway systems his greatest achievement.

According to a 1953 article from the *Chicago Tribune*, the first lady "looked with house-wifely horror at the faded draperies, the faded upholstery, the dingy color schemes" when she first entered the mansion. With no significant funding yet available to upgrade the decor, she "managed, like most housewives, by fixing up one room at a time." Recycling objects already in the mansion, she repaired attic furniture, re-cut and re-colored draperies, borrowed paintings from museum collections, and retrieved rugs that had been stored in the attic and on the ground floor. In the process of reupholstering furniture, she often discovered original fabrics and made an effort to return them to their earlier styles. The first lady also turned her attention to the grounds, enlarging the garden and replacing "random growth of scrubs . . . with more formal evergreen hedges, cannas, and tulips." Speaking to a reporter, the governor said, "We feel that the mansion belongs to the people. We want them to be able to see it without concealing underbrush.'"

While these modest improvements were underway, the state's senate was considering a large appropriation to renovate the mansion. One senator criticized the move, stating, "The mansion 'looks like a barn' and ought to be torn down." Despite this opinion, he ultimately joined his colleagues in voting for the appropriation. A complete overhaul of the mansion's antiquated electrical system was among the functional aspects of the refurbishment. Funds also became available for the first lady to conduct more comprehensive redecoration, with a focus on the state rooms.

On the first floor, a modern, neutral color scheme was carried out in the Northeast Parlor, with white wool rugs, cotton damask drapery with "a bold brown design on a cork background," and furniture upholstered in shades of cork, brown, and rust. Decorated in varied shades of green and furnished with blonde fruitwood chairs, the Northwest Drawing Room presented an equally unified palette. In another of the parlors, a serene palette of blue and gray complemented a richly colored Persian rug. While luxurious materials including satin, velvet, and silk were employed throughout the state rooms, the use of cotton and nylon subtly introduced a less formal sensibility. Traditional elements still found expression, however, particularly in the State Dining

Room, where Wedgwood-blue wallpaper figured with images of Greek ruins covered the walls.

The first lady also supervised the redecoration of the ground-floor rooms with a focus on family living. The room governors Green, Stevenson, and Stratton had used as their mansion office was transformed into a game room for listening to records and playing shuffleboard and ping pong—a favorite pastime of the governor. Another room, known as the Arizona Room, paid homage to the state where Stratton and his daughter Diane attended university. Wallpaper panels depicting cowboys and a Western-themed painting entitled *Bringing in the Strays* established the theme. In contrast with the refined textiles typically used at the mansion, the furniture was upholstered in roughly textured fabrics and the draperies were made of tweed. More formal materials were employed in the Chinese Room, a sitting room with furnishings inspired by an Asian painting that was a personal possession of the Strattons. In keeping with the painting's palette and the Asian theme, black lacquer woodwork and furniture contrasted with red Chinese silk wall coverings and red cushions. This and most of the other ground-floor rooms were designed to be converted into guest rooms, greatly increasing the mansion's capacity to host overnight visitors.

Accounts show that the Strattons entertained more frequently than many previous administrations. An estimated twenty-five thousand people were received at the mansion during each of their early years in the mansion. In addition to hosting large state gatherings, the first lady also organized entertainments for her daughters, including a "Coke-tail party" for Diane and a *Treasure Island*–themed party for five hundred young people. Visiting dignitaries included President Dwight D. Eisenhower and Vice President Richard Nixon, as well as an array of international leaders who came to the mansion—Liberian President William V. S. Tubman, Indonesian President Sukarno, West Berlin Mayor Willy Brandt, El Salvador President José María Lemus, Irish President Seán O'Kelly, and King Hussein of Jordan. When Queen Elizabeth II and Prince Philip came to Chicago in 1959 to mark the opening of the Saint Lawrence Seaway, the Strattons were among the greeting party and the governor rode in the motorcade with the queen.

PREVIOUS PAGES Governor and First Lady Stratton greet the public from the mansion's portico. Behind them the central staircase, soon to be returned to its original elliptical form, rises in a rectangular flight.

LEFT In 1889, the brick of the mansion was painted a light stone color intended to recall the exterior of the White House. It was subsequently repainted in a variety of light tones as seen in this photograph, taken during the Stratton administration, until its original appearance was restored in 1971.

ABOVE In 1955, First Lady Shirley Stratton sat for a portrait by Chicago artist John Doctoroff, known for his paintings and drawings of American presidents including one of Abraham Lincoln in 1936. Governor Stratton was so pleased with her portrait that he commissioned Doctoroff to paint one of himself.

RIGHT During the Stratton administration, relaxed family life was enjoyed in the mansion, particularly on the ground floor, which included a game room.

OPPOSITE The Stratton family's Great Dane strikes a pose in the mansion's stately stair hall.

ROYAL VISIT

Queen Elizabeth II and Prince Philip (seen above with Governor Stratton) traveled to Canada and the United States in 1959 for a forty-five-day journey during which the monarch christened the Saint Lawrence Seaway, a new passage linking the Great Lakes to the Atlantic Ocean. After arriving via Lake Michigan on the HMY *Britannia*, the royal pair traveled a short distance by barge before being greeted by Chicago Mayor Richard J. Daley and his wife, Governor and First Lady Stratton, and twelve ambassadors representing the British Commonwealth nations at Chicago's Queens Landing, so named in honor of the event. Ceremonial cannons blasted and "The Star-Spangled Banner" rang out as they arrived. The queen's thirteen-hour tour of Chicago continued with a motorcade procession down Michigan Avenue, with Governor Stratton and Mayor Daley riding with the queen in an open car showered by confetti. A visit to the International Trade Fair, where the queen traversed the longest red carpet in the world, and tours of the University of Chicago campus, the Museum of Science and Industry, and the Art Institute of Chicago prompted the monarch to remark, "Ever since we landed this morning, we have not ceased to be impressed by the massive dignity of your city. . . . We shall carry with us . . . a memory of the generous hospitality of Chicago, which will long warm our hearts."

OPPOSITE Dressed in formal attire, complete with opera-length gloves, First Lady Stratton prepares to meet Queen Elizabeth II during her 1959 visit to Chicago.

RIGHT In addition to receiving engraved invitations to a dinner honoring the queen, guests were provided a memorandum with suggestions for appropriate attire.

SUGGESTIONS FOR DRESS:

Dinner by the Mayor of Chicago and Mrs. Daley in honor of Her Majesty Queen Elizabeth II and His Royal Highness The Prince Philip, Duke of Edinburgh, in the Grand Ballroom of the Conrad-Hilton Hotel, Chicago, Illinois, July 6, 1959.

In response to many inquiries the Office of the Chief of Protocol, Department of State, has established the following guideline for dress for the dinner by the Mayor of Chicago in honor of Her Majesty Queen Elizabeth II in accordance with the usual customs regarding dress for state occasions in Washington during the summer months.

Proper attire for gentlemen is described as usual as "black tie." For the summer months this is considered as including for gentlemen white tuxedo jacket, black tie, and black tuxedo trousers. A black jacket is just as suitable for those who prefer not to wear a white jacket. Miniature decorations may be worn.

Mrs. Daley, the wife of the Mayor of Chicago, and Mrs. Stratton, the wife of the Governor of Illinois, will both wear full length evening dresses. It is anticipated that Her Majesty Queen Elizabeth II will wear a full length gown especially selected for the Chicago visit. The short length evening dress is considered equally correct. It is appropriate for ladies to wear decorations. It is understood that the Queen has no objection to ladies' wearing a black or decolleté dress.

Although the Queen has no strong feelings on the subject of gloves, she does prefer for ladies to wear gloves when they are being presented, especially when there are a large number of people. Short gloves should be worn for luncheon and long gloves for dinner.

Other Programs during the day will be informal. The gentlemen will wear dark business suits.

In honor of
Her Majesty Queen Elizabeth II
and His Royal Highness The Prince Philip
Duke of Edinburgh
The Mayor of the City of Chicago and Mrs. Richard J. Daley
request the pleasure of your company
at Dinner
on Monday, the sixth of July
at half after eight o'clock
The Grand Ballroom · Conrad Hilton Hotel

A reply is essential
before June 27th

This is not an Admittance Ticket

Although the Strattons were committed to inviting the public into the life of the mansion, the governor and first lady reluctantly abandoned the long-observed tradition of hosting a New Year's Day open house in 1957 due to a steady decline in attendance. A reporter from the *Illinois State Journal* expressed "a real twinge of disappointment [over] the passing of a long-standing tradition in Springfield," adding that "[t]he 'casual' way of living in general and the attraction of televised bowl games in particular are blamed for the demise of the custom." The frequency of events declined during the governor's second term, but the Strattons found a new way of interacting with their constituents in 1960, when they offered what would today be considered public tours, beginning a new chapter in mansion life.

Otto Kerner
Helena Cermak Kerner
(1961–1968)

Progressive Democrat Otto Kerner was elected as governor of Illinois at the beginning of America's 1960s cultural revolution. Born in Chicago, Kerner first served in the National Guard, then joined the U.S. Army during World War II and saw duty in the North African, Italian, and Pacific theaters. After retiring from the National Guard in 1954 as a major general, Kerner began his government career as a U.S. Attorney. As Illinois's governor, he promoted economic development, education, the arts, and equal access to jobs and housing. The landmark mental health programs he implemented became a model for national healthcare reform.

During Kerner's two terms, he succeeded in increasing foreign exports with the goal of promoting job growth in the state. He also won for Illinois a contract to build the Fermi National Accelerator Laboratory—a United States–owned particle physics laboratory still operating today. Kerner advocated policies that addressed race relations during a turbulent time of riots and violence. Following his time as governor, he became the chair of the National Advisory Commission on Civil Disorder, working to find solutions to racial division. Foreseeing the grave danger inequality posed to American cities, he summarized the committee's findings, stating, "Our nation is moving toward two societies, one black, one white—separate and unequal."

When Governor Kerner and First Lady Helena Cermak Kerner moved into the mansion in 1961, there was urgent concern about safety. An inspection found it to be "potentially quite a dangerous dwelling," and head of housekeeping staff Helen Van Diver told a journalist that she was "scared to death" by the place. Later that year, the governor approved an appropriation for fire-safety alterations, including a fire escape from the second floor, an alarm system, and a second-floor smokescreen. At the same time, the mansion's slate roof was replaced with asphalt tile. These improvements, however, were not sufficient to address deteriorating conditions, which prompted some legislators to propose a bill to sell it and construct a new one. The move was endorsed by state representa-

tives, who likened spending more money on the house to "throwing money down a rat hole," and warned against letting "our historical ideas carry us away."

Despite the dilapidation of the mansion, meetings and entertainments continued to take place in its rooms. The first lady told a reporter, "I don't like the mansion so much, because of the termites," but she continued to preside graciously over events, including a meeting about the creation of the Illinois Arts Council and receptions for guests such as Lincoln biographer and poet Carl Sandburg. President Lyndon B. Johnson's daughter attended a reception when she was in Springfield for a Young Citizens for Johnson rally. The first lady also hosted informal parties, including a Coke and punch party for young people participating in the Midwest Horse Fair.

In 1963, the Illinois House passed a bill to build a new Governor's Mansion, drawing the ire of those who advocated preservation of the nineteenth-century building. "They didn't tear down the White House just because it needed repairs," said Catharine Yates Pickering, granddaughter of Governor Richard Yates Sr. and daughter of Governor Richard Yates Jr. "I think the great historical value of the mansion is being treated lightly by the legislators." A group of concerned Illinoisians, including former First Lady Stratton, First Lady Kerner, and the wives of many other notable residents of Springfield formed a group to prevent the demolition of the mansion. Named in honor of a recent history of the mansion prepared by historian Octavia Roberts Corneau, the group was called the Mansion Manuscript Committee.

The lengthy and contentious discussion about the fate of the Governor's Mansion reflected contemporaneous discourse in America that pitted proponents of urban renewal against the nation's preservationists. Those in favor of urban renewal supported widespread demolition of entire swaths of cities such as Philadelphia and New York, including many historic buildings. Among the most shocking losses was New York City's original Pennsylvania Station, a stately building designed by the renowned firm of McKim, Mead & White, demolished in 1963. The destruction of that building heightened controversy about the fate of historic buildings. Kerner adopted a neutral position on the mansion, leaving the decision to other Illinois lawmakers. "I'm just passing through. That's something for the people to determine through the legislature."

In 1965, Kerner vetoed a bill appropriating 900,000 dollars for the mansion's renovation, citing fiscal concerns. However, in that same year, he approved a proposal from Representative Paul F. Elward for a new commission to study the condition of the mansion, described in contemporaneous newspapers as a "shanty" and a "slum." In addition to the architects, engineers, and historians who were consulted, participants also included former first ladies Green and Stratton, acting first lady Ives, and former governors Stevenson and Stratton. Among the concerns identified were collapsed ceilings, unsafe floors, substandard heating and air-conditioning and electrical systems, infestations of rats and termites, and threat of fire. The committee's report detailed options ranging from demolishing

the house and replacing it with an "all modern building of contemporary design," to preserving it in the manner of the 1949 to 1952 White House renovation, which retained as much historical character as possible while employing modern materials and technology as required.

Many who participated in and were consulted during the study were relieved with the finding that "the loss of a building of historical importance is not necessary as much of the present building is in sound condition." Rather than recommending demolition, the committee suggested that the mansion be preserved as a Victorian residence, noting, "The early Victorian style of the Executive Mansion has graceful elegance befitting the attendance of heads of government and their ladies." Having considered several design options to expand the mansion, commission members suggested reconfiguring it with one-story wings on the east and west sides that would accommodate garage and storage areas and a fallout shelter, topped with landscaped terraces visible from the first-floor state rooms. The commission also proposed replacing the kitchen-laundry addition on the south side with a three-story wing combining service functions and private quarters for the First Family.

This decision inspired Elizabeth "Buffy" Ives, former governor Adlai Stevenson's sister who acted as first lady during most of his administration, to write a lengthy letter to Representative Elward criticizing the proposed east and west wings as "a serious mistake" and taking issue with "garage stalls" that were practically part of the house, as well as the aboveground fallout shelter. However, she also wrote, "I am very, very happy that our unusual and charming Governor's home will be preserved. It is a distinguished house, and I, for one, heard its long whispers through the night from all those who had lived there through happy and sad periods."

In 1967, a bill to spend 1.5 million dollars on repairing and remodeling the mansion was approved, but a decision was made to delay the project until after Illinois's sesquicentennial celebration, by which time Kerner had resigned to accept an appointment to the U.S. Court of Appeals for the Seventh Circuit. Although the governor and first lady never enjoyed the opportunity to live in the improved mansion, the stage was set for a major remodeling to take place during the next administration.

PREVIOUS PAGES Governor Otto Kerner gathers with the first lady and their two children for a family portrait.

LEFT A 1970 photograph by renowned Chicago photographer Richard Nickel documents the metal-and-glass firewall installed on the second-floor landing during the Kerner administration, when efforts were made to mitigate dangerous fire hazards at the mansion.

RICHARD NICKEL

In 1970, photographer Richard Nickel (1928–1972) was invited to record for posterity the rooms of the Governor's Mansion just before the beginning of a major rehabilitation and renovation project that would greatly change their appearance. Born in Chicago to first-generation Polish Americans, the photographer developed an interest in architecture when walking near his childhood home on Logan Boulevard, a mansion-lined street later to become an official Chicago landmark. This experience sparked a lifelong passion for historic architecture. Exposed to photography at an early age by his father, an amateur photographer, Nickel later enrolled at the Illinois Institute of Design to study the art form. While there, he began photographing the buildings of Louis Sullivan. Upon witnessing the destruction of these and other historic structures during the urban renewal movement of the latter half of the twentieth century, he began campaigning for their preservation. When efforts failed to protect a building, Nickel photographed it inside and out to make a lasting record of its character and craftsmanship. He also salvaged distinctive architectural artifacts from doomed buildings, a practice that led to his death in 1972 when a portion of the old Chicago Stock Exchange building collapsed on him. Much of his work was published posthumously in a book titled *Richard Nickel's Chicago: Photographs of a Lost City*.

LEFT AND FOLLOWING PAGES
Richard Nickel's photographs captured the appearance of the Lincoln Parlor, Family Dining Room, West Parlor, and Music Parlor before the 1971–1972 renovation.

REBIRTH
AND
REJUVENATION
1970–2014

Richard B. Ogilvie
Dorothy Shriver Ogilvie
(1969–1973)

When Richard B. Ogilvie and First Lady Dorothy Shriver Ogilvie moved into the mansion in 1969, the recommendations of the 1967 Executive Mansion Commission's report, known as the Elward Plan, had not yet been enacted. In the meantime, the house's dangerous conditions and failing electrical, plumbing, and fire-proofing systems had worsened, making the house unsafe to inhabit. Debate concerning the commission's recommendations continued, at times heatedly. The suggestion that wings be added to the east and west sides of the mansion was particularly contentious. Both the governor and first lady objected to the idea. An editorial in the *Illinois State Journal* in April 1969 observed, "For months just about everyone has had his say about the Executive Mansion. There has always seemed to be something missing in this discussion and now it has become obvious what it was. Nobody apparently had consulted the first lady who will be living there once the renovation is completed."

By May, the Elward Plan was shelved, and the governor's office requested that yet another in-depth survey be conducted, this time by the Springfield architectural firm Graham, O'Shea and Wisnosky, which had recently participated in the reconstruction of the Old State Capitol. Like Elward's commission, this firm deemed the building, with minor exceptions, to be structurally sound. However, the new plan dispensed with the previous plan's east and west wings and instead advocated adding only one wing, to be located on

RIGHT A rendering prepared in 1970 by the Springfield architectural firm of Graham, O'Shea and Wisnosky details the changes the firm would bring to the mansion during the Ogilvie administration.

DOROTHY SHRIVER OGILVIE

While working as a secretary, Chicago native Dorothy Shriver (1922–2016) insisted her husband-to-be Richard B. Ogilvie pass the bar examination before they married in 1950, according to her obituary in the *Chicago Tribune*. She also supported her husband's decision to leave a career in law to enter the political arena. As first lady, Dorothy Ogilvie led a committee to oversee the Governor's Mansion restoration, rejecting suggestions of demolition and influencing its current form. According to her daughter, Elizabeth Ogilvie Simer, "She was very encouraging of that preservation and very proud of the result." Referring to the period when the Ogilvies moved out of the mansion during the renovation, the administration's budget director, John McCarter, later chair of the board of regents of the Smithsonian Institution, observed, "She was willing to forgo the trappings of the wife of the governor. . . . That was a measure of her, a measure of her modesty and no flamboyance." According to the *Chicago Tribune*, the first lady also focused her attention on the care of children with disabilities during her husband's administration, visiting state institutions and encouraging related community-based programs.

ABOVE Kirk Fischer, design consultant, worked closely with First Lady Ogilvie.

RIGHT Playing an active role in nearly all aspects of the 1971–1972 remodeling, the first lady (far right) made frequent site visits.

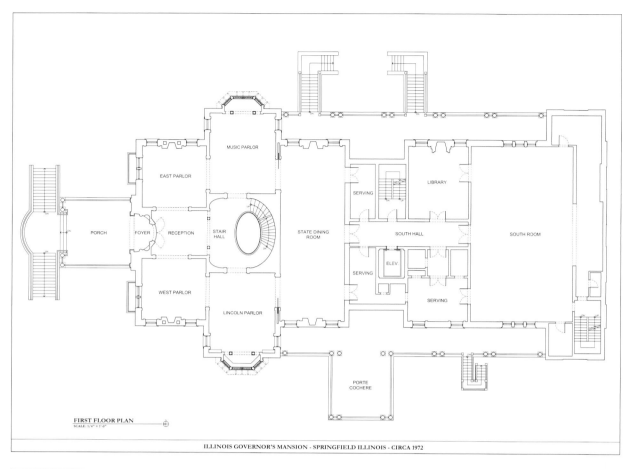

FIRST FLOOR PLAN
SCALE: 1/4" = 1'-0"

PORCH

FOYER

RECEPTION

EAST PARLOR

MUSIC PARLOR

WEST PARLOR

STAIR HALL

LINCOLN PARLOR

STATE DINING ROOM

SERVING

SERVING

SERVING

SOUTH HALL

LIBRARY

ELEV.

SOUTH ROOM

PORTE COCHERE

ILLINOIS GOVERNOR'S MANSION - SPRINGFIELD ILLINOIS - CIRCA 1972

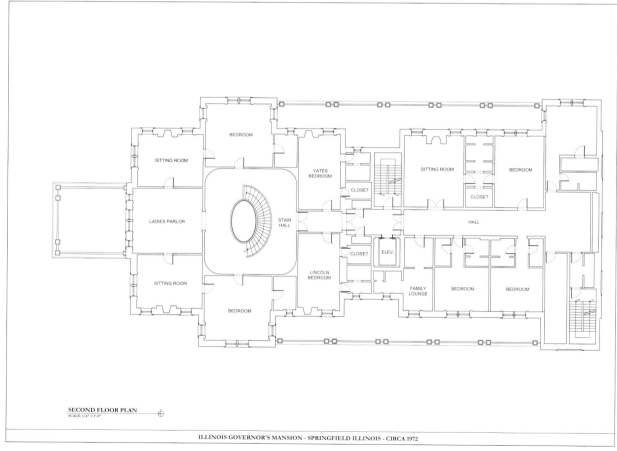

SECOND FLOOR PLAN
SCALE: 1/4" = 1'-0"

SITTING ROOM

BEDROOM

LADIES PARLOR

SITTING ROOM

BEDROOM

STAIR HALL

YATES BEDROOM

CLOSET

LINCOLN BEDROOM

CLOSET

ELEV.

SITTING ROOM

CLOSET

BEDROOM

HALL

FAMILY LOUNGE

BEDROOM

BEDROOM

ILLINOIS GOVERNOR'S MANSION - SPRINGFIELD ILLINOIS - CIRCA 1972

LOWELL ANDERSON AND JAMES T. HICKEY

When First Lady Ogilvie supervised the renovation and decoration of the Governor's Mansion, she engaged the services of two experts employed by the Illinois State Historical Library. Lowell Anderson served as the library's curator of historic sites and decorative arts advisor, and James T. Hickey as its Lincoln collection curator and historian. The first lady became acquainted with the two while they were reconstructing the Old State Capitol building. "One of the regular visitors to the building was the wife of the governor," Anderson recalled. "[S]he came to the Old Capitol frequently because she liked that kind of work. One day she came to the State Historian . . . and asked him if she could borrow the two men who were . . . responsible for the refurbishing of the Old Capitol. And he agreed. So Jim Hickey and I were loaned to the Executive Mansion to do the research." The pair took cues from the English Regency period for the decorations, primarily choosing drapery styles, wallcoverings, and furnishings within that aesthetic. According to Hickey, "We picked English Regency furniture not because it was ever used in the mansion, but because it is the type of furniture that goes very well with the Greek Revival interior." Anderson and Hickey also played a role in shaping the architectural features of the mansion. One of their most important contributions occurred when Anderson, working alongside the first lady, found tack marks that traced the arc of the 1855 elliptical stair.

ABOVE The key players in the renovation gathered for a photograph in the library in 1972. Back row: James T. Hickey, King V. Hostick (who had donated the bust of Lincoln), First Lady Ogilvie, Governor Ogilvie; front: Monte Holl (the woodworker who designed and fabricated the library), Lowell Anderson.

RIGHT Careful research allowed the architects to recreate faithfully the contours of the 1855 staircase.

OPPOSITE The 1971–1972 remodeling added a large wing to accommodate a library and spacious ballroom on the first floor and private family quarters above, while retaining the original room arrangement of the 1855 mansion structure.

the southern side, which would not exceed the east-west measurements of the 1855 structure. Following the example of the 1949 to 1952 renovation of the White House, the proposed alterations to the original structure were intended to preserve its character while taking advantage of modern materials and building technology.

While legislators debated an appropriations bill for the project, the specter of demolishing the building arose once again. "What's so historic about this building?" demanded one member of the House Appropriations Committee. "Did Lincoln sleep there

or something?" Supported by members of the General Assembly, the governor weighed in with the opinion that "the history of the 117-year-old structure was worth the added cost—a decision supported by the public approval given the . . . renovation of the White House." Further justifying the expense, Governor Ogilvie stated that in addition to accommodating the governor and his family, the mansion "should serve the dual role as a place to house visiting dignitaries" and "as a showplace attraction, a visual bit of Illinois's heritage." He further noted that the first lady would play an active

LEFT Workers employed a chemical
process to remove twenty-seven coats
of paint from the mansion's exterior
to avoid damaging the 115-year-old
Illinois-made brick.

ABOVE While surveying the renovation,
Governor Ogilvie confers with Illinois
art and architecture expert Jane Martin
Shair, who raised funds in Quincy for
furnishing one of the mansion's parlors.

role in the design to make sure that any changes were "authentic" and appropriate to the historic appearance of the mansion.

In December of 1970, preparations for the mansion's restoration and expansion finally began and the governor and first lady moved into temporary quarters in Springfield's Lincoln Tower, where portraits of Lincoln and Patrick Henry lent gubernatorial dignity to their apartment. In February 1971, the General Assembly appropriated 3,045,235 dollars for the project, which would be the first complete renovation in the building's history. The south wing, which had been built and added onto piecemeal since the 1885 addition of a kitchen wing during the Oglesby administration, was demolished and the replacement was erected. Larger than the previous wing, the new one was designed to complement the scale and appearance of the 1855 structure.

The architectural design included decorative elements intended to create a sympathetic relationship between the old building and the new addition. When a bracketed cornice inspired by the 1855 style was applied to the mansion, it was carried over to the new wing, creating a connection between the two. Porches connecting the two structures also enhanced visual harmony. In addition to the wing, the project called for significant changes to the mansion's exterior, intended to recall but not faithfully restore its original appearance. The most dramatic of these was the removal of twenty-seven coats of paint from the exterior, revealing the original red brick for the first time since it was painted in the 1880s. The project also called for dismantling the stone steps and porte cochère installed during the Tanners' remodeling. A new porch was built which, though it retained the split-stair configuration of the Tanner period, was stylistically inspired by the 1855 design.

The most significant change to the original structure's interior was the recreation of the elliptical stairway, replaced during the Tanner administration with a rectangular one. On the first floor, the mansion's State and Family Dining Rooms were joined to create a single formal dining room that spanned the entire south end of the house. On the second level, rooms originally intended primarily for family use were refurbished and repurposed for guests of state. These included four bedrooms, two sitting rooms, and a hall parlor. With the addition of the new south wing, a commercial kitchen as well as a family living and dining room could be accommodated on the ground floor. The first floor of the wing included a wood paneled library and a spacious area for large dinners, receptions, press conferences, and meetings. The second floor of the

LEFT This early 1990s photograph captures the warmth of the paneling expert woodworker Monte Holl of Decatur, Illinois, crafted for the south wing's library in 1972. Holl spent a year designing and installing the panels and mantel, which are composed of black walnut from the forests of southern Illinois.

NATIONAL REGISTER OF HISTORIC PLACES AND AMERICAN PRESERVATION MOVEMENT

Following the Ogilvie renovation, the Governor's Mansion was listed in 1976 on the National Register of Historic Places, the federal government's official list of sites, buildings, and objects considered worthy of preservation, established in 1966. One of the catalysts for the register's creation was the 1963 destruction of New York City's Pennsylvania Station. America's preservation movement has deeper roots, dating to the 1895 creation of the American Scenic and Historic Preservation Society and the 1853 Mount Vernon Ladies' Association, formed to restore and preserve George and Martha Washington's home. In 1921, citizens of Charleston, South Carolina, established the nation's first historic district, and in 1949, the National Trust for Historic Preservation was established to protect American historic places.

RIGHT A photograph taken in 1974 shows the deep portico with divided stairs and side porches as they looked after the Ogilvie renovation. These replaced the previous porch and stairs that were constructed in 1897 during the Tanner administration.

ZUBER & CIE WALLPAPER

When Anderson and Hickey turned their attention to what was then called the "ladies' sitting room," later the Kankakee Room, they selected Zuber & Cie wallpaper from a dealer in Chicago but lacked the 5,000 dollars to pay for the French scenic paper. In his memoir, Anderson recalled, "Two years later the ladies of Kankakee came up with a check for slightly over seven thousand dollars and they gave it to Mrs. Ogilvie to spend for the Mansion." When Anderson returned to Chicago to purchase the wallpaper, he discovered that the price had gone up to 7,000 dollars. Before installing it, he had the panels laminated on both sides "so that we could take it off the wall if necessary to repair the walls." When First Lady Pritzker renovated the room in 2019, it became evident that the plasticizing process had undermined the integrity of the wallpaper. Selecting the same pattern as Anderson, Les Vues d'Amérique du Nord, she donated new panels of Zuber wallpaper to replace those previously installed and expanded the wallcovering to include all the walls of the sitting room.

ABOVE A 2011 photograph documents the Kankakee Room's laminated Zuber & Cie wallpaper as it would have looked following its installation in the early 1970s.

RIGHT The panoramic scenes depicted in Zuber's woodblocked wallpaper have enjoyed popularity in Europe and America since 1797. A detail of the paper, replaced by First Lady Pritzker in 2019, conveys America's natural beauty.

addition created private family quarters, including bedrooms, a sitting room, and a kitchenette. The decoration of the mansion's interior, largely funded through donations and gifts from the people of Illinois, was conducted under the supervision of James T. Hickey and Lowell Anderson, curators and decorative arts experts employed by the Illinois State Historical Library.

Despite a delay caused by an elevator workers' strike, the project was completed nearly on schedule and in April 1972, the governor and his family moved back to the mansion, where finishing touches were being completed. Once settled, the governor continued his practice of conducting state business in the Capitol, breaking with the practice of previous governors such as Bissell, Horner, Stevenson, and Shapiro, who had worked largely from the mansion. A reporter for the *Illinois State Journal* commented on this change early in Ogilvie's administration, writing, "He apparently accepts the theory that the voters like to think of the governor going to work every day at the Statehouse, rather than operating at a suspected more leisurely pace at home."

During and after the renovation, Ogilvie pursued a broad agenda, including the institution of Illinois's first state income tax to address a severe fiscal situation, a record increase in state aid to public education, and modernization of the state's penal system. In addition, he initiated legislation to combat urban decay and to establish the Illinois Environmental Protection Agency to safeguard air and water resources, which became a model for the federal Environmental Protection Agency. Before his election, Ogilvie had a decade-long history of combating organized crime, and as governor, he established the Illinois Bureau of Investigation, known as the state's "little FBI." After the end of his term, Ogilvie was awarded the Order of Lincoln—the state's highest honor—by his successor, Governor Daniel J. Walker. Before leaving office, he issued an executive order providing for use of the mansion as a historic site under the curation of the Illinois State Historical Library.

James R. Thompson
Jayne Carr Thompson
(1977–1991)

James R. Thompson came to prominence as an Illinois Republican in the 1970s when, as U.S. Attorney for the Northern District of Illinois, he successfully prosecuted several dozen Chicago politicians for corruption, including former governor Otto Kerner. Many of those he helped convict were members of the Democratic organization headed by Mayor Richard J. Daley. Although Thompson was presented by his party to run against Daley for mayor of Chicago, he declined, soon afterward announcing his candidacy for governor instead. Though Thompson lacked government experience, he had powerful speaking skills and an excellent memory for names and faces. These characteristics helped him win the gubernatorial election of 1976, defeating Democratic Secretary of State Michael Howlett, who had Daley's support, with sixty-five percent of the vote.

JAYNE CARR THOMPSON

Jayne Carr Thompson (1946–) led a groundbreaking career as a woman working in Illinois's legal system. After graduating from the Northwestern University School of Law as one of only thirteen women in a class of 125 students, she became the Illinois assistant attorney general. She prosecuted many cases, including one argued before the U.S. Supreme Court. Later, she became co-chair of the state's prosecution assistance bureau, traveling to numerous counties to aid attorneys investigating and trying criminal cases. When her husband, James R. Thompson, was elected governor of Illinois, she was on track to become chief of the criminal division, but concerns about conflict of interest interrupted the promotion. During her early years as first lady, Jayne Carr Thompson worked for a Springfield law firm. "Many people in Springfield were disconcerted about the fact that I was not devoting myself full time to official duties as first lady," she recalled. "They worried 'Who's going to serve the tea?'" When her daughter, Samantha, was born, Thompson resigned to spend time with her. She was actively involved with social service organizations as chairperson of a task force addressing health issues for infants and children and the needs of working families and co-chair of the Chicago Cancer Society's 1980s fundraising crusade. She also supported the work of Illinois's Women's Business Development Center. She resumed law practice following the end of her husband's administration.

OPPOSITE In a portrait painted by William Chambers in 1993, Governor James R. Thompson, wearing an Illinois-made watch, stands before a likeness of Abraham Lincoln that came from his personal collection.

Known as Big Jim, the 6-foot-6-inch Thompson was to become Illinois's longest serving governor, winning four consecutive terms.

Not surprisingly, legal reform was an important piece of Thompson's agenda. As governor, he signed a bill reinstating the death penalty for multiple categories of murder. The death penalty was later abolished in 2011 by Governor Patrick J. Quinn. In step with national get-tough-on-crime attitudes, Thompson shifted the focus for certain crimes from rehabilitation to punishment, resulting in Illinois building more prisons than at any other time in state history. A pragmatic moderate known for establishing coalitions with Democrats, Thompson passed a number of more left-leaning bills, including legislation granting government employers and teachers collective bargaining rights and establishing a compounding three-percent cost-of-living increase for retirees from Illinois government jobs, including schoolteachers. When controversial right-to-work legislation was being considered by the General Assembly, the governor invited union representatives and members over for an informal gathering at the mansion to defuse the situation. First Lady Jayne Carr Thompson recalled arranging for a beer truck and portable toilets with next to no notice for the impromptu gathering, which drew hundreds of men who walked from the Capitol to the mansion's lawn.

Throughout Thompson's fourteen-year stint as governor, the state's fiscal wellbeing faltered due to structural shifts in the nation's economy, particularly the loss of industrial jobs in the Midwest. By his second term, ongoing declines in the manufacturing sector led Illinois to be considered a Rust Belt state. To counter the trend, Thompson energetically implemented strategies designed to attract and maintain businesses and to shore up the state's job and tax base. His accomplishments included luring Diamond-Star Motors to locate in central Illinois and successfully convincing Sears, the state's largest private-sector employer, and other locally based companies to stay. Thompson also opened overseas trading missions with the goal of expanding the export economy for Illinois products and traveled to Japan and Europe to promote Illinois as a potential site for industrial investments. On the local front, when the Chicago White Sox threatened to leave the state, the governor pressured the legislature to provide a publicly financed stadium. He also supported the restoration of Navy Pier to promote Chicago's economy and quality of life.

Thompson was ahead of his time in recognizing art and historic architecture as avenues for promoting tourism and economic development. Among his achievements was the creation of the Art-in-Architecture program, in which one-half of one percent of all public building construction costs were designated for original works of art to be publicly displayed. In 1985, he established the Illinois Historic Preservation Agency to improve educational and recreational programming at the state's historic sites. The agency also managed applications to the National Register of Historic Places. To build awareness of the state's rich craft heritage, he advocated for the creation of the Illinois Artisans Program, which established shops in Chicago and southern Illinois promoting the

BARTELS HAND-CARVED FURNITURE

In 1879, German immigrant William H. Bartels (1848–1932) began carving elaborately decorated wood furniture in his Carthage, Illinois farmhouse, initially using wood from a rail fence. Later, he worked with white oak said to have been reclaimed from the Nauvoo Mormon temple in Hancock County. Most Mormons were driven out of Illinois by 1846, and the temple was destroyed by fire and storm. Bartels's designs were as local as his materials, with motifs of ferns, wild roses, and oak leaves abounding. Bartels gained international fame during the 1893 World's Columbian Exposition in Chicago, when his work was displayed in the Illinois State Building's governor's rooms, which were open to the public except when Governor John P. Altgeld was entertaining dignitaries in them. After the fair, the furniture was returned to Bartels, and it remained in his possession until his death in 1932. It was then purchased by his friend, Illinoisan Arthur Black. Three decades later, the furniture returned to public view when Black's widow loaned it to the Illinois State Museum. When Black's estate came up for auction in 1980, members of the Executive Mansion Association, led by Governor James R. Thompson, purchased it for 40,400 dollars. Today, the collection furnishes a bedroom and sitting room that pay tribute to the vision and talent of an exceptional Illinois artist.

OPPOSITE A pair of stone sphinxes facing the East Garden were acquired during the Thompson administration.

ABRAHAM LINCOLN PRESIDENTIAL LIBRARY AND MUSEUM

The Abraham Lincoln Presidential Library opened in 2004, with the associated museum welcoming its first visitors a year later. Within two years, attendance reached one million, increasing to five million by 2022. Funding came from public and private sources, including Illinois schoolchildren, who contributed pennies to reach a tally of 47,000 dollars. Planning was spearheaded by Governor Jim Edgar, who believed there should be a library dedicated to Lincoln in Springfield, where the president spent most of his life. The institution's central mission is collecting, preserving, and interpreting the life and times of Abraham Lincoln and Illinois history. The museum combines an artifact collection with immersive exhibits and the library encompasses approximately twelve million documents, including letters, diaries, books, and pamphlets. When then-Senator Barack Obama spoke at the opening, he observed, "We come to celebrate not a building but a man. And as that man called once upon the better angels of our nature, so is he calling still, across the ages, to summon some measure of that character, his character, in each of us, today."

OPPOSITE A nineteenth-century painting of George Washington on horseback bearing the signature of Harry Roseland (circa 1867–1950) hangs in the ballroom.

work of state artisans. In addition to the two original shops, two more sites were opened at the Illinois State Museum in Springfield and the Dickson Mounds Museum Store in Lewistown. Under Thompson's administration, the state also purchased the DuQuoin fairgrounds, adding a second state fair location.

A much-loved, flamboyant character, Thompson enjoyed participating in parades and was known for skidding down the giant slide at the Illinois State Fair in a T-shirt, once accompanied by his dog. He also enjoyed performing as a livestock auctioneer during the fair, and he rode a horse in the Capitol. During his travels across the state, Thompson often stopped into antiques shops to indulge in his hobby of collecting, which he termed "pickin' and junkin'." In 1979, when an elaborately carved suite of furniture crafted in the late-nineteenth century by Illinois artisan William H. Bartels came up for auction, Thompson spearheaded the effort to raise private funds to purchase it. Exhibited in the 1893 World's Columbian Exposition's Illinois State Building, the historic furniture now graces one of the bedrooms in the Governor's Mansion. Thompson was also a strong advocate for the state's 1981 purchase and rehabilitation of Springfield's Frank Lloyd Wright–designed Dana-Thomas House. In 1985, the state government's administrative Chicago headquarters building, considered one of the city's most significant postmodern structures, was renamed in honor of the governor. In 1991, Thompson's successor, Governor Jim Edgar, presented him with the Order of Lincoln.

Jim Edgar
Brenda Smith Edgar
(1991–1999)

When Illinois Secretary of State Jim Edgar was elected Illinois's thirty-eighth governor in 1990, he inherited a fiscal crisis brought on by excessive government spending during the high-flying 1980s. To meet the formidable challenge of a 200-million-dollar shortfall, he initiated a number of cost-saving programs, including instructing agencies to cut millions from their budgets. Slashing jobs in his own office, he saved nearly one million dollars. Although he refused to raise income taxes to solve the state's problems, he made permanent a Thompson-era two-year income tax surcharge and called for increases in so-called "sin taxes" on sales of alcohol. Despite Edgar's efforts, the state's budget continued to suffer from the ill effects of the 1990s recession, according to Tom Schafer's 1998 history, *Meeting the Challenge: The Edgar Administration, 1991-1999*. While struggling to repair the state's fiscal situation by reducing government spending, Edgar pursued priorities such as education, child welfare, and the protection of needy citizens.

When he announced his candidacy for re-election in fall of 1993, according to Schafer, he pointed to the fact that Illinois had survived an unprecedented budget crisis. "But we didn't downsize the take-home pay of hardworking taxpayers," Edgar stated. "Instead we downsized government." Edgar's budgetary victories were hard-won, often leading to lengthy and contentious debate within the General Assembly. When he underwent emergency quadruple-bypass surgery at the time of one such debate, he called in four days later to urge a compromise. Edgar's hard work paid off in his run for reelection, which he won by the second widest gubernatorial vote margin in Illinois history, exceeded only by Governor Thompson's 1976 victory. During his second term, the governor continued his agenda of reducing government spending and supporting education, calling for an increase of one billion dollars in state aid to schools. Edgar also focused on initiatives designed to promote Illinois's heritage and increase cultural tourism.

The governor achieved what may be his greatest and most lasting legacy when he rallied legislative support for the creation of a Lincoln presidential library and museum in Springfield. "There had been talk of establishing a center in Springfield to tell the full story of Lincoln since at least 1990, but the necessary funding never materialized," wrote a reporter from the *State Journal Register* in 1998. In 1996, the legislature had passed an appropriation of 2.3 million dollars for the project, but the amount was not released, as necessary matching private funds were not raised. Two years later, Edgar led the General Assembly to allocate 4.9 million dollars to begin planning for what would become today's Abraham Lincoln Presidential Library and Museum.

At the 1998 Abraham Lincoln Association banquet, Edgar told a crowd of three hundred people, "It's crucial for other generations to know this great man and what he has meant to this nation and what he still means to this nation." In 2010, five years after the museum's opening and six years after the library's, Edgar reflected, "I think it has proven to be everything we had hoped, if not more, and . . . has been a huge attraction to Springfield—not only the museum, but the activities that go on." The governor added, "The museum . . . draws the most people, but the library is the important part of keeping up the research and having it available for scholars." During his time in office, Edgar also continued a program begun under the Thompson administration to catalog more than 100,000 documents related to the president's legal career and to digitize them, making them available online.

In another program designed to call attention to the state's rich history, Edgar initiated plans to update the Illinois State Museum's Dickson Mounds facility in Lewistown. Addressing public controversy about the site's display of the remains of Native people, Edgar worked with representatives of Native nations to develop an interpretive facility that respected their concerns. In 1994, Edgar visited the facility to celebrate the opening of the new state-of-the-art exhibitions. Another initiative spurred the creation of a new center interpreting the westward expedition led by Meriwether Lewis and William Clark, which began from nearby Camp Dubois on May 14, 1804. The facility became the centerpiece of the state's 2004 bicentennial commemoration of the expedition.

The governor also turned his attention to the state's rich agricultural heritage and the annual Illinois State Fair. In 1991, with fiscal reform in mind, he directed the fair's managers within the

ABOVE In 1994, Governor and First Lady Edgar pose with their dogs, Emy and Daisy, beside the southern Illinois governor's residence located on the DuQuoin State Fairgrounds, one of the two residences provided for the governor's use.

BRENDA SMITH EDGAR

First Lady Brenda Smith Edgar (1948–) initiated several programs focusing on the wellbeing of children, women, and families. In 1991, she launched Project HEART (Helping to Ease Adoption Red Tape) intended to increase interest in adoption, create partnerships with private sector employers to encourage adoptions, and improve access to health insurance for adoptive families. At the time the program was announced, 370 children, many of them ethnic minorities and children with special needs, were awaiting adoption. She also dedicated energies to a campaign called Help Me Grow designed to help new mothers raise healthy children and promote preventative health care and safety. Among the organization's initiatives was a program to give teddy bears to children taken into protective custody by the Department of Children and Family Services. Looking toward the future, Brenda said, "It's important for me to have some time to think and . . . reinvent my life after politics. . . . I would just love to grow some flowers. I think it would be very interesting."

Illinois Department of Agriculture to cut waste and inefficiency and become more self-supporting by raising revenue and enlisting corporate support. Insisting that "the fair provide good, clean, quality entertainment and education," he asked for a greater number of free and family-oriented attractions. After the 1998 event, an article in the *State Journal Register* reported that the "fair finally reflects Edgar's family-oriented goals." The piece quoted the governor as declaring, "We've achieved what we wanted. . . . [T]here are all kinds of things for a family to do." Prohibiting the consumption of alcohol outside beer tents on the fairgrounds, as well as at the mansion and Capitol complex, were among the governor's other "clean living" policies.

Marking the centennial of the fair's permanent location in Springfield in 1894 (previously the fair had moved from place to place throughout the state), major improvements were made to the fairgrounds. A new two-story, air-conditioned livestock center was built, a historic barn was saved from demolition, and improvements were made to the grandstand and Junior Livestock Building. Events included the Governor's Sale of Champions, an auction benefitting the Future Farmers of America, the 4-H Foundation, and young exhibitors' college educations. At the start of each Illinois State Fair, Edgar inspected the fairgrounds on horseback. During his administration, annual attendance averaged nearly 750,000, including a peak of 826,600 visitors in 1998.

Bruce V. Rauner
Diana Mendley Rauner
(2015–2019)

Bruce V. Rauner came to the Illinois governorship without previous political experience. He had a background in finance and was previously chairman of one of Illinois's largest private equity firms. Through the work of First Lady Diana Mendley Rauner, he delivered on a campaign promise to restore the Illinois Governor's Mansion as a metaphor for the great state it graces. Soon after her husband's inauguration, the first lady took up the mission with zeal, organizing a meeting of architectural experts to plan the scope of the renovation. These included John Vinci, principal of Chicago's Vinci Hamp Architects. The first lady also revived the Illinois Executive Mansion Association, bringing together leaders from across the state to raise private funds and offer expertise. The team included businessman, art scholar, philanthropist, and preservationist John Bryan; Joseph Gromacki,

LEFT The West Parlor, as it appeared in 2011 during the Governor Patrick Quinn administration, featured nineteenth-century furnishings and windows layered with curtains, shirred lances, and upholstered cornice boards.

a lawyer with expertise in historic preservation, arts, and antiques; and Leslie Hindman, founder and president of one of the nation's largest auction houses. With the first lady as the committee's chair, they raised roughly fifteen million dollars from Illinois corporations and individuals.

Upon seeing the mansion for the first time, the first lady's impression was that it resembled a haunted house, with crumbling iron fences overgrown with shrubs and trees that hid the darkened building from view. As she looked at it, she formulated a new vision for a building like the White House, where people would walk or drive by and look across the lawn to see a well-lit, beautifully restored house and say with pride, "That's our Governor's Mansion." Once sufficient funds were raised, the committee began to bring this vision into reality. The first order of business was finding an architectural firm that could meet the various challenges the project posed—particularly formulating an approach to renovating the 1855 mansion, which had been modified at various times over a 160-year period. "Vinci Hamp Architects was the obvious choice, given the strong vision and support John Vinci expressed from day one," the first lady said. The firm was known for its work preserving and adapting historic buildings, including several designed by Frank Lloyd Wright. It had handled restoration of the architect's home and studio in Oak Park, Illinois, and renovated the Illinois State Capitol and the Art Institute of Chicago.

The first priority was to address major structural damage to the house, which suffered from a leaking roof, molding walls, rotting wood, and a host of other problems caused by decades of deferred maintenance. Afterwards, attention was focused on aesthetic issues, particularly how best to unify the disparate periods expressed in the mansion's appearance. One question was how to bridge the Italianate aesthetic of the 1853 John Mills Van Osdel design with the Victorian-era 1897 remodeling conceived by George H. Helmle. Another issue was what to do with the well-meaning but somewhat ill-conceived efforts made during the 1970s expansion to recreate mid-nineteenth-century style design elements and integrate them into the substantial new wing. There was also discussion about removing Helmle's mansard roof to expose the original cupola buried within, but it was determined that the roof needed to remain because the building's modern mechanical equipment was installed beneath it. Ultimately, principal architect Phil Hamp decided that the preponderance of evidence, including period photographs and surviving original construction, suggested returning the house largely to its circa 1900 appearance, while including details emphasizing the original mid-nineteenth-century plan.

This involved recreating some of the handsome elements of the 1897 design, including stamped metal cornices and a rooftop balustrade. Unlike the late nineteenth-century portico, however, which included a double flight of stairs, the new portico emulates the single flight of steps Van Osdel designed in 1855. Although neither the steps nor the porch to which they ascend adhere strictly to either period, the intent and the materials employed are sympathetic to both. While looking backward for inspiration, the architects also embraced modern technologies and building codes. "Our goal was to bring the mansion back in many ways to its historical appearance while also bringing it up to modern building standards, with LEED energy efficiency and modern accessibility code compliance," said Hamp.

LEFT In 2018, Governor and First Lady Rauner presided over the opening of the mansion following a four-year-long renovation planning and construction process.

OPPOSITE Vinci Hamp Architects employed stamped zinc decoration to reproduce the appearance of the pressed metal cornice molding of the Tanner era.

The challenge of how best to marry the 1970s wing with the old mansion raised more questions about respecting the various stages of the mansion's history. In 1972, when the wing was added, the architects sought to unite the two structures visually and stylistically with elements that blurred the past with the present. When a cornice with brackets that were neither Italianate nor Victorian was added to the original mansion, it was carried over to the roofline of the new addition. In the Vinci Hamp design, this was removed from both structures and a recreation of Helmle's 1897 cornice was installed along the roofline of the old mansion. The 1972 remodeling had also included a pair of two-story verandas that linked the two structures in an attempt to create continuity. The Vinci Hamp firm decided to remove these elements, explaining that "the project was about letting the bones of the original building stand out and making a distinction between the original 1855 building and the 1972 addition."

Significant renovation took place within the mansion as well. Walls and ceilings suffering from water damage were removed; many areas were taken down to the studs. Bryan and Gromacki worked with Vinci Hamp to shape decisions about what the remodeled interior should look like, consulting with historic preservation experts to develop a plan. "We did a tremendous amount of research, finding old photos that helped us determine how the rooms had been furnished at different periods in the house's history," Gromacki recalled. "As a result, we were able to determine original elements of the interior architecture, which made it possible for the architects to recreate them." Bryan and Gromacki also succeeded in identifying sources for historic reproduction wallpaper and carpeting that were compatible with the house's history and made recommendations for furnishings consistent with the project's aims. "Our goal was to recognize the continuity of history over the course of the building's existence, but at the same time bring to life certain important historic elements of the interior spaces," Gromacki noted. "We more or less returned it to a late-1890s appearance."

Two of the original mansion's second-floor suites were redecorated to celebrate significant periods in Illinois history. One was designed to celebrate the 1893 World's Columbian Exposition in Chicago—an important high point in Illinois's cultural history. The room was furnished with a collection of bedroom and parlor furniture carved by Illinois artisan William H. Bartels that was exhibited at the fair, and decorated with William Morris reproduction wallpaper and light fixtures coinciding with the period. A second themed room named the Governor's Suite featured furnishings and artifacts relating primarily to the administrations of governors Yates Sr. and Oglesby and the Civil War and Reconstruction periods of the 1860s and 1870s. A third room decorated with furnishings said to have been used by or given to Abraham Lincoln was dedicated to the president. The room across the hall with childhood artifacts and ephemera from first families told the stories of the children who grew up in the mansion. These rooms, which were open to the public, reflected the first lady's wish that the house serve an educational purpose, offering a direct way of communicating the story of Illinois through historic objects. "Period rooms offer opportunities to make history come alive," she said.

With most of the service functions transferred to the south wing, the ground-floor rooms received the most dramatic remodeling, including the addition of a room dedicated to the history of the mansion that served as the orientation site for public tours. This floor, as well as the ones above, also offered display space for an exhibition entitled *Art of Illinois: An Exhibition of Fine and Decorative Arts Presented in the People's House*. Created by the first lady with fine art curator Wendy Greenhouse, decorative arts curator Sharon S. Darling, Bryan, Gromacki, and Hindman, the exhibition featured works of art, craft, and decorative art by centuries of Illinois artists and craftspeople. The mansion's family quarters in the south wing also received significant remodeling and updating. Designed for a time when the first families who lived there were attended by staff providing their meals, the wing's living quarters had no serviceable kitchen. Instead, the first family was expected to dine on the ground floor, near the commercial kitchen. The ground-floor level also included a family living room. In the renovation, a fully functioning kitchen was installed on the second floor, along with an adjoining family dining area, complementing the existing bedrooms and living room.

With fundraising and research beginning in January 2015 and construction starting in May 2017 and completed in May 2018, the Rauner administration renovation transpired remarkably quickly. Coinciding with the bicentennial of Illinois's statehood, the house opened to the public in July 2018 with a weekend-long open house. The *Art of Illinois* exhibition debuted in the mansion at the same time. "That [these works] arrive at this 200th birthday moment for the state is a fitting start to the next life of a home that, in its newest iteration, earns its place among Illinois Historic Places as The People's House," First Lady Rauner wrote in her foreword to the exhibition's catalog. "With this recent renovation, the goal was . . . expansive. We wanted to bring Illinois into the home in ways that had not been envisioned in past renovations. We saw the Mansion as both residence and symbol, the latter of Illinois statesmanship, inclusion, and hospitality."

OPPOSITE A view of the Rauners' remodeling of the mansion as seen from the second-floor landing of the elliptical staircase.

THESE PAGES First Lady Rauner's redecoration
of the mansion involved the creation of several
period rooms, including the Columbian Exposition
Room (above) with its collection of William
H. Bartels furniture and the Governor's Suite
(opposite) with furniture from the Civil War era.

III

SETTING
THE
TABLE

THE
ILLINOIS STATE
CHINA

In 1873, First Lady Helen Judson Beveridge ordered the first commissioned set of state china from French porcelain producer CH. Pillivuyt & Cie. The hand-painted service featured an interpretation of the 1868 state seal: an eagle holding in its beak a banner bearing the words "State Sovereignty" and "National Union." It perches on an orb inscribed "1818"—the year in which Illinois became the twenty-first state. The tureen is the only surviving piece. In 1971, First Lady Dorothy Ogilvie worked with artisans at Illinois's Pickard China company, conferring with its designers to produce a new official state service for use in the Governor's Mansion. The design boasts a wide etched-gold rim with a garland pattern surrounding the state seal, also in gold.

Founded in 1893 in Edgerton, Wisconsin, by former cut-glass and artware salesman Wilder A. Pickard and his wife, Minnie, Pickard China moved to Chicago in 1905 with a staff of fifty, many of whom represented the city's diversity of highly trained immigrant European artisans. These craftspeople developed their own hand-painted patterns, including flora, landscapes, and birds. In 1911, the company introduced etched-gold pieces with gold borders like those in the Ogilvie service and all-over gold treatments. In the latter part of the twentieth century, Pickard China's reputation for fine artisanship gained national and international attention, garnering prestigious government commissions for the White House, the U.S. Capitol dining room, Camp David, Air Force One, and American embassies, as well as from Queen Elizabeth II.

PREVIOUS PAGES First Lady Pritzker's oak-leaf patterned soup bowls complement the gold-rimmed state china created for First Lady Ogilvie in the early 1970s. Both services were manufactured by the Antioch, Illinois-based Pickard China company.

RIGHT A hand-painted tureen produced in France by CH. Pillivuyt & Cie in 1873 is the only remaining piece of Illinois's first official china, commissioned by First Lady Beveridge.

LEFT A cabinet lined with Italian marbled paper holds state china, including First Lady Ogilvie's gold-rimmed charger with a contemporary coordinating mug in the upper left corner. The remaining plates are from the service First Lady MK Pritzker designed with the Pickard China company.

ABOVE A Meissen platter hand-painted
with violets and green leaves is a piece
from one of Mary Todd Lincoln's
services. It holds slices of the almond flour
cake she favored that was named for her,
which is still served at the mansion today.

OPPOSITE Dessert plates with an oak tree
and leaf motif share the table with a
silver tea service and napkins bearing
the Illinois state seal. The remaining two
pieces on the table are part of the U.S.S.
Illinois silver service.

In 2020, First Lady Pritzker collaborated with Pickard China to create a twenty-first-century Illinois state service inspired by Mary Todd Lincoln's china pattern. Violets, the state flower, decorate the borders of the dessert plates and centers of the coffee saucers. Leaves and acorns of the white oak, the state tree, form the decorative motif of the soup bowls and borders of the dinner plates, and a fully depicted oak graces the center of each salad plate. This new pattern was designed to coordinate seamlessly with the existing patterns in the mansion's collection. Still family owned, Pickard is the last remaining American fine china manufacturer whose products are entirely made in the United States.

Table settings for state dinners are not complete without the gleam of silver to contrast with the gold rims of china. There are several patterns of flatware in the mansion's collection but the most magnificent and complete comes from the U.S.S. *Illinois* service (1943–1945), which includes dinner forks, salad forks, seafood forks, place spoons, cream-soup spoons, demitasse spoons, iced-tea spoons, and individual butter spreaders. A pair of sterling silver candelabras engraved with the state seal from the same service often illuminates the State Dining Room's long table, accompanied by holloware urns brimming with flowers.

ABOVE In 1911, the Pickard China company introduced wide bands of etched gold to add luster to its designs. The chargers designed by MK Pritzker feature this embellishment, along with the state seal in the center. In order to accommodate the scale of modern china, these are larger than the Ogilvie chargers.

OPPOSITE The large seated Lincoln portrait in the ballroom is a 1939 copy by Catherine Carter Critcher, commissioned by Jessie Lincoln Randolph, a daughter of Robert Todd Lincoln. Robert had purchased the 1869 original and praised it on multiple occasions, once calling it "the best portrait of my father existing." It was bequested to the people of the United States through the will of Robert's widow, Mary Harlan Lincoln, and now hangs in the State Dining Room at the White House.

ABOVE A base of dolphins in the Venetian style supports a highly decorated blue-and-white faience punchbowl.

OPPOSITE The sterling silver punchbowl crafted by Illinois fabricators C. D. Peacock for the U.S.S. *Illinois* between 1943 and 1948 and subsequently given to the mansion serves as an elegant container for floral arrangements.

FOLLOWING PAGES Holiday china featuring ribbons and garlands made by Illinois's Pickard China company adds a festive touch to a table set for Christmas in the Governor's Dining Room, located on the ground floor of the mansion.

ABOVE The Pritzkers continue the tradition of celebrating Passover at the mansion annually with members of the Jewish community. A contemporary silver kiddush cup with a gold-plated interior is from their personal collection.

RIGHT The work of award-winning, Israel-based Judaica silversmith Sari Srulovitch has been the subject of many international exhibitions. She brings original, contemporary design elements to traditional ceremonial pieces, including the seder plate she designed for the state of Illinois, donated by the Pritzkers to the people of Illinois.

FOLLOWING PAGES Bright flowers wait in a service room to be arranged in some of the mansion's many silver, crystal, and china vessels.

IV

THE
SOCIAL
CALENDAR

Ever since 1856, when Governor and First Lady Matteson hosted an open house for Springfield citizens to see the newly constructed dwelling, the Governor's Mansion has been the center of the capital city's social life. The public has long been invited to events, including a New Year's Day reception—an event held annually until the advent of televised football games that day led to its demise. For decades, it was a tradition for the ladies of Springfield to call on the first lady during Wednesday At Home parties. Military units and veterans frequently gathered on the grounds, and during World War II, soldiers came to USO parties featuring big band music and dancing.

The mansion's grounds were a regular site for events, including military band concerts that were popular in the early 1900s and antiques fairs hosted by late-twentieth century Governor Jim Thompson. In 1918, they provided the backdrop for the Illinois Centennial Celebration, during which President Theodore Roosevelt stayed at the mansion and attendees viewed a costumed pageant with historical themes. For more than a century, costuming has been a recurring motif, ranging from an 1880s Charles Dickens-themed party and 1902 Daughters of the American Revolution reception featuring colonial-era attire to today's Halloween celebrations, during which governors and first ladies dress in costume to hand out candy to trick-or-treaters.

During the Stratton administration in the late 1950s, it was estimated that twenty-five thousand people passed through the mansion's doors yearly. In 1960, First Lady Stratton started a new chapter in the mansion's history by opening its doors to tours. Although its mission is a public one, the mansion also serves as a private home, hosting family events like wedding ceremonies and receptions, birthday celebrations for young children, and teenage parties, including a "Coke-tail" party for Governor Stratton's daughter Diane in 1955.

Christmas has long been celebrated at the mansion with decorations decking the portico and the parlors. On the grounds, lights and a Christmas tree and more recently a menorah share the holiday spirit with passersby. The first known seder at the mansion was celebrated during the Thompson administration and Passover is still commemorated today. While providing a place for festivities, the mansion also offers solace and hope during somber times, as witnessed by the Covid memorial installed on the front lawn in 2021. No events took place at the mansion at the height of the pandemic. Whether solemn or glad, all these activities invite citizens from Illinois and beyond into the welcoming embrace of the People's House.

PREVIOUS PAGES During parties, an upholstered bar on wheels transforms an alcove off the State Dining Room into a beverage serving area. A member of the mansion staff, Thad Rebbe, is seen behind the bar.

LEFT Illinois is recognized as the pumpkin capital of the world. In October, gourds of many shapes, sizes, and hues offer autumn color to the mansion's grounds.

'TIS THE SEASON

ABOVE A gold menorah from the Pritzkers' personal collection graces the mantel in the West Parlor in recognition of Hanukkah in 2022.

OPPOSITE The rooms of the mansion are open for public tours during the holiday season, where a twenty-foot-tall tree decorated with bows and balls reaches towards the top of the stair hall and delights visitors.

ABOVE AND RIGHT Holiday decorations in a palette of white and gold unified the West Parlor, Lincoln Parlor, and State Dining Room in 2022, emphasizing the rooms' harmonious flow. Springfield volunteers help deck the halls.

PREVIOUS PAGES In 2022, matching
Christmas trees flanked the mantels at
either end of the State Dining Room,
where a profusion of winter greenery
arranged in the U.S.S. *Illinois* silver punch
bowl served as an elegant centerpiece.

ABOVE Decorated with ornaments ranging
from Ferris wheels to representations of
Abraham Lincoln, corn dogs, and deer
(the state animal), the library's Christmas
tree was an homage to all things Illinois.

OPPOSITE Trees in the ballroom honored
Illinois's first responders, members of
the military, and soldiers who have died
in the line of duty.

THIS PAGE Dancers from the Springfield Youth Performance Group pose in costumes from *The Nutcracker* at a 2022 party for donors and sponsors of the Springfield Memorial Foundation to kick off the Memorial Holiday Fest.

OPPOSITE An illuminated menorah and a thirty-foot Christmas tree decorate the grounds of the mansion during the holiday season.

THIS PAGE AND OPPOSITE The grounds of the mansion have long opened to Springfield's youth for seasonal parties and entertainments. Today, they are a centerpiece of the city's Halloween celebration, during which the governor and first lady hand out candy in costume to more than one thousand children a year. In 2019, they dressed as *Star Wars* characters (upper left), and, in 2022, as Superman and Wonder Woman (opposite, lower left).

HONORING AN ICON

THIS PAGE AND OPPOSITE In 2019, the Governor's Mansion was the site of the eighty-fifth birthday party for Jesse White, the longest serving Illinois secretary of state, as well as the first Black American elected to the position. The party featured a performance by the Jesse White Tumblers, a group formed by White in 1959 to provide a positive alternative for inner-city youth. Before entering public service, White served as a paratrooper in the 101st Airborne Division and played for the Chicago Cubs. Legendary funk musician George Clinton (opposite) entertained the crowd.

ILLINOIS COVID MEMORIAL

ABOVE AND OPPOSITE On March 16, 2021, one year following the first known Covid-19 death in Illinois, an installation opened on the mansion grounds honoring Illinoisans who had died from the disease since the onset of the pandemic. The installation included 102 pairs of wings representing Illinois's counties that together held more than 5,500 ribbons. Each ribbon represented approximately four Illinoisans who lost their lives to the virus. The ribbons were illuminated by glowing spheres commemorating victims of the pandemic, while also representing the permanence of light in the darkest of times. Illinoisans were invited to pay tribute to their loved ones by tying ribbons at the perimeter of the installation.

of mourning – as individuals, as families, as communities and as a state – is a step toward healing. In
truth, First Lady MK Pritzker commissioned this installation to pay tribute to the more than 23,000
o died from COVID-19 across our 102 counties, as represented by 102 sets of wings. Together, the
over 5,500 ribbons, each representing 4 Illinoisans who lost their fight with this virus. The glowing
keep the ribbons shining through the night, serve as a reminder to always remember the victims of
pandemic, while also representing the permanence of light even in the darkest of times.
rom March 16th, 2021 – the one-year anniversary of the first known COVID-19 death in
, 2021, the one-year anniversary since Governor Pritzker directed all flags be lowered at
e who lost their lives to COVID-19.
Governor invite all Illinoisans, whether or not they are able to come bear witness at the
me to honor their neighbors, loved ones, and fellow Illinoisans who died in the COVID-19
membrance that we will forge forward as one Illinois, committed anew to a shared vision
all.

SNAPSHOTS
FROM THE
SOCIAL
SCRAPBOOK

ABOVE The portico of the mansion has witnessed many celebrations over the years including a 1910s family gathering for the wedding portrait of Governor Edward Dunne's daughter.

LEFT Governor Louis Emmerson's granddaughter celebrates her birthday with friends in the State Dining Room in the 1930s.

THIS PAGE Clockwise from top: Members of Sigma Delta Pi gather at a tea hosted by First Lady Shirley Stratton in the 1950s; for the 1918 Illinois centennial celebration, Governor and First Lady Lowden's daughter, Florence, (second from left) poses in the Masque of Illinois pageant, flanked by women representing England, Belgium, Colombia, and France; Governor and First Lady Thompson and their dogs take a break from mansion life in the 1980s to coast down the giant slide at the Illinois State Fair; Governor Adlai E. Stevenson II with the Sisters of the Holy Family of Nazereth standing on the mansion drive in 1952; Governor Henry Horner and companions set off for a sleighride from the mansion portico on New Year's Eve, 1939.

OPPOSITE The front of the mansion was the setting for USO dance parties for servicemen during Governor Green's administration as seen in 1943 (top) and in 1944 (bottom), which featured hula dancers as entertainment.

ABOVE In 1902, First Lady Helen Wadsworth Yates created a festive atmosphere during the Christmas season with Japanese lanterns festooned with Spanish moss, and gasoliers and a candelabra garlanded with greenery.

OPPOSITE A 1950s photograph captures Governor William Stratton and his family in an intimate moment as they hang tinsel on their Christmas tree.

FORMER GOVERNORS
AND
FIRST LADIES

1818–1822	Shadrach Bond	Achsah Bond
1822–1826	Edward Coles	—
1826–1830	Ninian Edwards	Elvira Lane Edwards*
1830–1834	John Reynolds	Catherine Manegle Reynolds
1834 (served fifteen days)	William L. D. Ewing	Caroline L. Berry Ewing*
1834–1838	Joseph Duncan	Elizabeth Smith Duncan
1838–1842	Thomas Carlin	Rebecca Huitt Carlin
1842–1846	Thomas Ford	Frances Hambaugh Ford
1846–1853	Augustus C. French	Lucy Southworth French
1853–1857	Joel A. Matteson	Mary Fish Matteson
1857–1860	William H. Bissell	Elizabeth Kane Bissell*
1860–1861	John Wood	Ann M. Streeter Wood
1861–1865	Richard Yates Sr.	Catharine Geers Yates
1865–1869	Richard J. Oglesby	Anna White Oglesby
1869–1873	John M. Palmer	Malinda Ann Neely Palmer
1873 (served ten days)	Richard J. Oglesby	—
1873–1877	John L. Beveridge	Helen Judson Beveridge
1877–1883	Shelby M. Cullom	Julia Fisher Cullom
1883–1885	John M. Hamilton	Helen Williams Hamilton
1885–1889	Richard J. Oglesby	Emma Gillett Keays Oglesby
1889–1893	Joseph W. Fifer	Gertrude Lewis Fifer
1893–1897	John P. Altgeld	Emma Ford Altgeld
1897–1901	John R. Tanner	Cora Edith English Tanner
1901–1905	Richard Yates Jr.	Helen Wadsworth Yates
1905–1913	Charles S. Deneen	Bina Day Maloney Deneen
1913–1917	Edward F. Dunne	Elizabeth J. Kelly Dunne
1917–1921	Frank O. Lowden	Florence Pullman Lowden
1921–1929	Lennington Small	Ida Moore Small
1929–1933	Louis L. Emmerson	Ann Mathews Emmerson
1933–1940	Henry Horner	—
1940–1941	John H. Stelle	Wilma Wiseheart Stelle
1941–1949	Dwight H. Green	Mabel Kingston Green
1949–1953	Adlai E. Stevenson II	Ellen Borden Stevenson (divorced 1949)*
1953–1961	William G. Stratton	Shirley Breckenridge Stratton
1961–1968	Otto Kerner	Helena Cermak Kerner
1968–1969	Samuel H. Shapiro	Gertrude Adelman Shapiro
1969–1973	Richard B. Ogilvie	Dorothy Shriver Ogilvie
1973–1977	Daniel J. Walker	Roberta Dowse Walker
1977–1991	James R. Thompson	Jayne Carr Thompson
1991–1999	Jim Edgar	Brenda Smith Edgar
1999–2003	George H. Ryan	Lura Lynn Lowe Ryan
2003–2009	Rod R. Blagojevich	Patricia Mell Blagojevich
2009–2015	Patrick J. Quinn	—
2015–2019	Bruce V. Rauner	Diana Mendley Rauner

For more than a century and a half, Illinois's first ladies (seen opposite in chronological order) have devoted their time and attention to the welfare of the state's citizens, spearheading efforts to improve quality of life, while also supporting the work of their husbands.

*Images not shown.

NOTES AND CREDITS

HISTORY OF THE PEOPLE'S HOUSE
Joel A. Matteson (pages 92–103)
"A Card," *Illinois State Journal*, January 26, 1853, 3.

James T. Hickey, ed., "An Illinois First Family: The Reminiscences of Clara Matteson Doolittle," *Journal of the Illinois State Historical Society* 69, no. 1 (February 1976): 10.

No title, *Illinois Daily Journal*, May 25, 1853, 3.

John T. Stuart, Springfield, January 13, 1856, to Bettie Stuart, Stuart-Hay Family Papers, Abraham Lincoln Presidential Library.

John G. Nicolay notes of June 24, 1875, conversation with John T. Stuart, in Michael Burlingame, ed., *An Oral History of Abraham Lincoln: John G. Nicolay's Interviews and Essays* (Carbondale: Southern Illinois University Press, 1996), 14.

William H. Bissell (pages 103–04)
"Festivities at the Executive Mansion," *Daily Illinois State Journal*, February 16, 1857, 3.

Thomas J. McCormack, ed., *Memoirs of Gustave Koerner, 1809–1896*, vol. 2 (Cedar Rapids: The Torch Press, 1909), 40.

William H. Bissell, Belleville, January 2, 1857, to Abraham Lincoln, Abraham Lincoln Papers, Library of Congress.

"The Land of the Illini; No. 7," *Chicago Daily Tribune*, December 29, 1895, 32.

"Woman Tells of Time She Locked Lincoln Outside," *Rockford Republic*, July 19, 1919, 2.

John Clayton, *Illinois Fact Book and Historical Almanac 1673–1968* (Carbondale: Southern Illinois University Press, 1970), 107.

Dan Monroe, *At Home with Illinois Governors: A Social History of the Illinois Executive Mansion 1855–2003* (Springfield: Illinois Executive Mansion Association, 2002), 16.

"'The Last of Earth,'" *Chicago Press and Tribune*, March 23, 1860, 3.

Richard Yates Sr. (pages 104–15)
"The City. Inauguration of Hon. Richard Yates, Governor Elect of the State of Illinois," *Daily Illinois State Journal*, January 14, 1861, 3.

"The Governor's Levee," *Daily Illinois State Journal*, February 11, 1862, 1, reprinted from the *St. Louis Missouri Republican*, January 31, 1862, 3.

John H. Krenkel, ed., *Serving the Republic—Richard Yates, Illinois Governor and Congressman Son of Richard Yates, Civil War Governor: An Autobiography* (Danville: The Interstate Printers and Publishers, Inc., 1968), 2–5.

"The Closing Scenes at Springfield," *New York Daily Tribune*, May 8, 1865, 5.

Richard J. Oglesby, first term (page 115)
"The Closing Scenes at Springfield," *New York Daily Tribune*, May 8, 1865, 5.

"Reception of Gen. Grant," *Daily Illinois State Journal*, September 13, 1865, 3.

"Reception and Dinner to the 29th U.S. Colored Regiment," *Daily Illinois State Journal*, November 23, 1865, 3.

"Grand Masquerade Party," *Daily Illinois State Journal*, March 1, 1867, 4.

John M. Palmer (pages 115–17)
"Springfield," *Chicago Republican*, September 23, 1869, 1.

"Horse-and-Buggy-Days Ball," *Illinois State Journal*, August 17, 1937, 6.

"Fred. Douglass," *Illinois State Journal*, January 26, 1872, 2.

"Gov. Fifer's Home," *Chicago Tribune*, January 6, 1890, 1.

Richard J. Oglesby, third term (pages 117–22)
No title, *Illinois State Journal*, December 13, 1885, 8.

"Gov. Oglesby's Tree for the Children," *Chicago Daily Tribune*, December 26, 1886, 2.

"A Famous Artist," *Daily Illinois State Journal*, July 12, 1888, 4.

"Personal," *Illinois State Journal*, July 16, 1888, 4.

"Art and Artists," *Chicago Sunday Inter Ocean*, January 6, 1889, 13.

"Dickens' Disciples," *Illinois State Journal*, February 17, 1885, 8.

Joseph W. Fifer (pages 122–27)
"Messenger Gorum Buried," *Chicago Daily Inter Ocean*, July 3, 1890, 5.

"Gov. Fifer's Home," *Chicago Tribune*, January 6, 1890, 1.

Florence Fifer Bohrer, undated recollections, box 4, Octavia Roberts Corneau Papers, Abraham Lincoln Presidential Library.

"The Executive Mansion," *Chicago Daily Inter Ocean*, February 16, 1889, 12.

"The Executive Mansion," *Illinois State Journal*, December 21, 1889, 1.

"The Executive Mansion," *Chicago Daily Inter Ocean*, January 6, 1890, 7.

"Fair Exhibits," *Daily Illinois State Register*, September 14, 1889, 1.

John P. Altgeld (pages 127–30)
Robert P. Howard, *The Illinois Governors: Mostly Good and Competent Men* second ed., rev. and updated Peggy Boyer Long and Mike Lawrence (Springfield: Institute for Public Affairs, University of Illinois at Springfield, 1999), 159–68.

"Women Register," *Illinois State Journal*, October 17, 1894, 4.

"Reception at Executive Mansion," *Illinois State Register*, May 17, 1895, 8.

"All for Education," *Illinois State Journal*, December 27, 1895, 6.

"Governor's House," *Chicago Sunday Inter Ocean*, January 16, 1898, 33–34.

"Is Now Organized," *Illinois State Journal*, November 14, 1896, 5.

"Governor's Reception," *Illinois State Register*, November 14, 1896, 5.

"Salvation Army Dinner," *Illinois State Register*, December 25, 1896, 5.

"Governor's House," *Chicago Daily Inter Ocean*, January 16, 1898, 34.

John R. Tanner (pages 133–36)
"Soldiers Reviewed at the Mansion," *Illinois State Journal*, May 3, 1898, 2.

"Mrs. Tanner on Lynchings," *Chicago Daily Inter Ocean*, April 28, 1899, 7.

"Revenue Bills Up," *Illinois State Journal*, April 22, 1897, 2.

"Governor's House," *Chicago Sunday Inter Ocean*, January 16, 1898, 34.

"It Will Be Stately," *Illinois State Journal*, August 25, 1897, 4.

"Mansion All Aglow," *Illinois State Journal*, December 17, 1897, 6.

John Thomas Trutter and Edith English Trutter, *The Governor Takes a Bride: The Celebrated Marriage of Cora English and John R. Tanner, Governor of Illinois* (Carbondale: Published for the Illinois State Historical Society by Southern Illinois University Press, 1977), 23.

"Will Be Repaired," *Springfield Sunday Journal*, June 13, 1897, 4.

Journal of the House of Representatives, Fortieth General Assembly (Springfield: H. W. Rokker, State Printer and Binder, 1897), 673.

Richard Yates Jr. (pages 136–46)
"Governor Is Serenaded," *Illinois State Journal*, July 11, 1901, 5.

"Invitation of Mrs. Yates," *Illinois State Journal*, February 24, 1901, 4.

"Calendars Cleared," *De Kalb Daily Chronicle*, May 7, 1901, 3.

"Gov. Yates and the Minority," *Illinois State Register*, January 8, 1903, 4.

"Mrs. Yates in Her New Home," *Chicago Daily Tribune*, January 16, 1901, 2.

"Yates Receives Eighth," *Illinois State Register*, August 6, 1903, 8.

"Cold House for Gov. Yates," *Chicago Daily Tribune*, February 18, 1903, 2.

"Executive Mansion Is Garbed in Elaborate Floral Dress," *Illinois State Journal*, June 5, 1903, 2.

Charles S. Deneen (pages 146–53)
"Governor has a Close Call," *Illinois State Register*, June 3, 1907, 7.

"Sylvester Here Today," *Illinois State Register*, April 23, 1907, 7.

"Hold Service at Mansion," *Illinois State Journal*, March 13, 1909, 5.

"Suffragettes Hold Meeting," *Illinois State Register*, March 30, 1909, 5.

"Reception to the Y.W.C.A.," *Illinois State Register*, April 30, 1910, 7.

"Via Christi Class at Mansion," *Illinois State Register*, October 18, 1910, 7.

"Two Hundred Suffragettes Invade the Capitol," *Illinois State Register*, March 8, 1911, 9.

"Among the Art Galleries," *Chicago Inter Ocean*, December 8, 1912, 50.

Frank O. Lowden (pages 153–57)
"Lowden in Answer to His Defamers," *Rockford Daily Register-Gazette*, August 24, 1920, 5.

"Executive Mansion is Beautiful by the Many But Simple Decorations," *Illinois State Journal*, November 4, 1917, pt. 2, 1.

"Seventy-five Women Attend 'At-Home' at the Executive Mansion," *Illinois State Register*, January 24, 1918, 5.

Florence Lowden Miller and Florence Pullman Lowden, extracts from diaries, box 5, Octavia Roberts Corneau Papers, Abraham Lincoln Presidential Library.

"Local Boy Thinks Teddy Fine Man," *Illinois State Journal*, August 30, 1918, 13.

"Frank O. Lowden and Miss Florence Pullman," *New York Times*, March 22, 1896, 26.

Henry Horner (pages 157–62)
Thomas F. Schwartz, "More pleasure in the pursuit than the possession," *Illinois Historical Journal*, 83 (Winter 1989), 263–70.

Thomas B. Littlewood, *Henry Horner and His Burden of Tragedy* (Bloomington, IN: Author House, 2007).

Dwight H. Green (pages 162–66)
"Governor's Mansion Here Will Undergo Extensive Repairs," May 4, 1941, *Illinois State Register*, pt. 2, 5.

Laws of the State of Illinois, Sixty-first General Assembly (Springfield: 1941), vol. 1, 197.

"Repair Work on Executive Mansion Nears Completion," *Illinois State Journal*, October 29, 1941, 7.

"New Year's Greetings Extended to Hundreds of Callers by State Officials at Executive Mansion," *Illinois State Journal*, January 2, 1942, 1.

"Seek 16 Million for State Defense," *Illinois State Journal*, December 16, 1941, 1.

"State House Static," *Illinois State Journal*, January 2, 1942, 5.

"Gov. Green to Give Broadcast Series," *Illinois State Journal*, February 26, 1943, 18.

"Colored Republican Women to Have Tea," *Illinois State Journal*, October 14, 1944, 5.

Adlai E. Stevenson II (pages 166–72)
"Governor's Sister to Aid at Reception," *Illinois State Journal*, December 30, 1949, 22.

"Governor Greets 1000 at Mansion," *Illinois State Journal*, January 2, 1950, 10.

Elizabeth Ives, notes of interview, box 5, Octavia Roberts Corneau Papers, Abraham Lincoln Presidential Library.

Porter McKeever, *Adlai Stevenson: His Life and Legacy* (New York: William Morrow Co., 1989), 203.

William G. Stratton (pages 172–80)
Joan Beck, "Living on a Budget in the Governor's Mansion," *Chicago Sunday Tribune Magazine*, December 13, 1953, 24–25, 40.

"State House Briefs," *Illinois State Journal*, March 24, 1955, 28.

Beulah Gordon, "Drawing Rooms at Illinois Executive Mansion Retain Elegance and Grand Manner of Days Before Civil War," *Illinois State Journal*, November 18, 1955, 5.

Beulah Gordon, "23 Governors Have Resided in Mansion First Occupied 100 Years Ago This Month," *Illinois State Journal-Register*, November 20, 1955, 8.

Beulah Gordon, "Two Rooms in Illinois Executive Mansion Are Used as Special Meetings for Young People," *Illinois State Journal*, November 27, 1955, 10.

"Oriental Room and Office of Social Secretary at Illinois Executive Mansion Pictured," *Illinois State Journal*, November 26, 1955, 18.

"Will Bypass Traditional Open House at Mansion," *Illinois State Journal*, December 15, 1956, 1–2.

Dan Monroe, *At Home with Illinois Governors: A Social History of the Illinois Executive Mansion 1855–2003* (Springfield: Illinois Executive Mansion Association, 2002), 122–23.

Otto Kerner (pages 180–83)

Robert P. Howard, *The Illinois Governors: Mostly Good and Competent Men* second ed., rev. and updated by Peggy Boyer Long and Mike Lawrence (Springfield: Institute for Public Affairs, University of Illinois at Springfield, 1999), 279–85.

Donald Lenhausen, "Reveal Fire Hazards in Executive Mansion," *Illinois State Journal*, March 14, 1961, 1.

"New Mansion Proposal Is Approved by House," *Illinois State Journal*, June 20, 1963, 1.

"Democrats," *Illinois State Journal*, August 16, 1963, 3.

"Funds Approved to Repair Mansion," *Illinois State Journal*, July 3, 1963, 7.

"Gov. Yates' Granddaughter Starts Fight to Save Mansion," *Illinois State Journal*, June 20, 1963, 50.

"Build New Mansion," *Rockford Morning Star*, July 25, 1965, 10.

"Senate Cuts Gas Tax Hike to 1c," *Illinois State Journal*, June 30, 1967, 4.

Report to the Illinois General Assembly by the Executive Mansion Commission with Recommendations for Action (Springfield: Illinois Executive Mansion Commission, 1967), n.p.

Richard B. Ogilvie (pages 190–204)

Dan Monroe, *At Home with Illinois Governors: A Social History of the Illinois Executive Mansion 1855–2003* (Springfield: Illinois Executive Mansion Association, 2002), 138–40.

"Mrs. Ogilvie Speaks Up," *Illinois State Journal*, April 12, 1969, 6.

Pauline L. Telford, "What Is 'Historic?'" *Illinois State Journal*, May 3, 1970, 19.

"Brief History of the Executive Mansion," undated, Illinois Executive Mansion Association Papers, Abraham Lincoln Presidential Library.

Lowell E. Anderson, interview by Melinda Kwedar, 1984, interview LIB 144, transcript, Oral History Collection, University Archives, University of Illinois at Springfield.

Graydon Megan, "Dorothy Ogilvie, Former Illinois First Lady, Dies," *Chicago Tribune*, December 16, 2016, n.p.

The Art of Illinois (Springfield: Illinois Governor's Mansion Association, 2018), 42.

James R. Thompson (pages 204–9)

Robert P. Howard, *The Illinois Governors: Mostly Good and Competent Men*, second ed., rev. and updated by Peggy Boyer Long and Mike Lawrence (Springfield: Institute for Public Affairs, University of Illinois at Springfield, 1999), 312–22.

Jim Edgar (pages 209–13)

Meeting the Challenge: The Edgar Administration 1991–1999 (Springfield: State of Illinois, Office of the Governor, 1998).

Lesley Rogers and Doug Pokorski, "Edgar: We Need Library for Lincoln," *State Journal-Register*, February 13, 1998, 1, 8.

Christopher Wills, "Fair Finally Reflects Edgar's Family-Oriented Goals," *State Journal-Register*, August 23, 1998, 18.

"Our Opinion. State Fair Left Lots of Great Memories," *State Journal-Register*, August 27, 1998, 4.

Jim Edgar, interview by Mark DePue, November 8, 2010, Volume V (Sessions 23–26), # ISG-A-L-2009-019.23, interview # 23, Abraham Lincoln Presidential Library.

EVERY EFFORT HAS BEEN MADE TO TRACE COPYRIGHT HOLDERS OF MATERIAL IN THIS BOOK.

The publisher gratefully acknowledges the considerable assistance and many historical photographs, architectural renderings, and print material provided by the Abraham Lincoln Presidential Library and Museum: pages 9, 10–11, 24–25, 26, 38, 84, 90–91, 94, 94–95, 98, 100–1, 101, 103, 109, 110–11, 118, 125, 127, 128–29, 132–33, 134, 135, 136, 140, 140–41, 141, 142–43, 145, 148–49, 148, 150–51, 154, 156, 160–161, 164, 165, 170–71, 173, 174–75, 176, 177, 178, 181, 190–91, 195, 196–97, 197, 200–1, 209, 258–59, 259, 262, 263

Photographs by Michael Mundy: pages 4, 12, 16, 19, 22, 27, 28–29, 32, 34–35, 36–37, 39, 40–41, 42–43, 44, 45, 46–47, 48–49, 50–51, 54, 56–57, 58, 62–63, 64–65, 66–67, 70, 70–71, 72–73, 75, 78–79, 82, 83, 85, 113, 126, 208, 218, 219, 220, 227, 236–37, 268, front and back covers

Photographs by Scott Shigley: front endpaper, pages 2–3, 14, 18, 20–21, 30, 31, 52, 53, 55, 60, 60–61, 68, 68–69, 69, 74, 76–77, 80–81, 96, 102, 105, 106–7, 108–9, 112, 116, 119, 123, 139, 144, 147, 155, 158, 168–69, 202–3, 206, 207, 215, 222–23, 224–25, 226–27, 228, 229, 230, 231, 232–33, 234, 234–35, 238, 240–41, 242, 243, 244, 244–45, 246–47, 248–49, 249, 251, 270–71

Floor plans by Adam Adamczyk: pages 97, 98, 99, 137, 138, 194

Endpapers: Front: Albert Meyer, Portrait of Abraham Lincoln, oil on canvas, circa 1925. On loan from the Abraham Lincoln Presidential Library and Museum; Back: Illinois State Archives

Pages 6–7: Photograph of Theodore Roosevelt, Governor Richard Yates Jr. and family, October, circa 1901. Library of Congress #2013651251

Page 8: Photographic portrait of Frederick Douglass, photograph by George Kendall Warren. Special Collections, Fine Arts Library, Harvard College Library, ©President and Fellows of Harvard College

Page 59: Left: Photograph of Frances A. Elkins, photographer unknown. Courtesy of David S. Boyd; right: photograph of Samuel A. Marx, ©Chicago Historical Society, published on or before 2015, all rights reserved. HB-07198. Chicago History Museum, Hedrich-Blessing Collection

Page 86: George P. A. Healy, Portrait of Governor Richard J. Oglesby, 1864. Courtesy of the Illinois Department of Natural Resources

Pages 88–89: Architectural rendering. Martin Burns/Stephen Chrisman with Ferguson & Shamamian Architects

Page 93: George Wright, Portrait of Governor Joel A. Matteson, 1861. Courtesy of the Illinois Secretary of State

Page 114: Above left: Portrait of Governor Richard J. Oglesby. Courtesy of the Illinois Secretary of State; above right, bottom left, and bottom right: photographs of Governors John M. Palmer, Joseph W. Fifer, and John P. Altgeld. Courtesy of the Abraham Lincoln Presidential Library and Museum

Page 118: Franklin Tuttle, Portrait of First Lady Emma Gillett Keays Oglesby and Jasper Oglesby, 1888. On loan from the Abraham Lincoln Presidential Library and Museum

Page 119: Franklin Tuttle, Portrait of John and Richard Oglesby. Executive Mansion Collection

Pages 120–21: *"The first dynamite bomb thrown in America"* May 4th. Chicago, IL, 1886, published by the Inter Ocean Co. Library of Congress #2008680516

Page 121: Notice, Chicago History Museum, ICHi-006214

Page 122: Photograph by Carlo Gentile of Frederick Douglass. Chicago History Museum, ICHi-010140

Page 124: *Lindsay Loved His Springfield Home*, Paper Booklet by Elizabeth E. Graham. Courtesy of the Illinois State Library

Pages 129: Photograph of First Lady Gertrude Lewis Fifer; **149:** Photograph of Clarence Liggins. Courtesy of the McLean County Museum of History, Bloomington, IL

Page 131: Ralph E. Clarkson, Portrait of Governor John P. Altgeld, 1898. On loan from the Illinois State Historical Society, photograph by Mark L. Johnson

Page 151: Photograph. Sangamon Valley Collection, Lincoln Library, Springfield's Public Library

Pages 152–53: Photograph. Chicago History Museum, ICHi-182734

Page 154: Photograph. Courtesy of the Washtenaw County Historical Society

Page 157: Alice Kellogg Tyler, Portrait of Jane Addams, oil on canvas, 1892. Jane Addams Hull-House Museum, University of Illinois at Chicago

Page 158: Floyd Brackney, Portrait of Governor Henry Horner. Executive Mansion Collection, photograph by Scott Shigley

Pages 158–59, 192, 192–93, 198–99, 265: Photographs. Executive Mansion Collection

Pages 162–63: Photograph of First Lady Mabel Kingston Green, March 9, 1942. ©*The State Journal*, USA TODAY NETWORK

Page 166: Photograph of Governor Adlai E. Stevenson II. Bettmann via Getty Images

Page 167: *Adlai E. Stevenson for President*, published by Volunteers for Stevenson

Page 168: Photograph by Mark L. Johnson

Page 179: Left: Photograph. Courtesy of the Abraham Lincoln Presidential Library and Museum; right: invitation and memorandum. Chicago Public Library, Harsh Research Collection, Abbott-Sengstacke Family Papers, Box 248 Folder 4

Pages 182–83: Illinois Executive Mansion, second floor, Stair Hall, Springfield, IL, 1853–1855. John Van Osdel, Richard Nickel, photographer. Richard Nickel Archive, Ryerson and Burnham Art and Architecture Archives, Art Institute of Chicago. Digital file #201006_221028_004

Pages 184–85: Illinois Executive Mansion, first floor, Living Room, Springfield, IL, 1853–1855. John Van Osdel, Richard Nickel, photographer. Richard Nickel Archive, Ryerson and Burnham Art and Architecture Archives, Art Institute of Chicago. Digital file #201006_221028_001

Page 185: Richard Nickel, self-portrait, Chicago, IL, circa 1950. Richard Nickel Archive, Ryerson and Burnham Art and Architecture Archives, Art Institute of Chicago. Digital file #201006_161213_001

Page 186: Illinois Executive Mansion, first floor, Dining Room, Springfield, IL, 1853–1855. John Van Osdel, Richard Nickel, photographer. Richard Nickel Archive, Ryerson and Burnham Art and Architecture Archives, Art Institute of Chicago. Digital file #201006_221028_003

Page 187: Illinois Executive Mansion, first floor, Living Room, Springfield, IL, 1853–1855. John Van Osdel, Richard Nickel, photographer. Richard Nickel Archive, Ryerson and Burnham Art and Architecture Archives, Art Institute of Chicago. Digital file #201006_221028_002

Pages 188–89: Illinois Executive Mansion, first floor, Music Room, Springfield, IL, 1853–1855. John Van Osdel, Richard Nickel, photographer. Richard Nickel Archive, Ryerson and Burnham Art and Architecture Archives, Art Institute of Chicago. Digital file #201006_221028_010

Pages 202, 212–13: Photographs, Matt Ferguson FergyPIX.com

Page 204: Photograph. UPI

Page 205: William Chambers, portrait of Governor James R. Thompson, 1993. Courtesy of the Illinois Secretary of State

Pages 210–11: Photograph of Governor Jim and First Lady Brenda Edgar, by Mars Cassidy. Eastern Illinois University, Jim Edgar Archives

Pages 214, 216, 252 (above right, bottom left, and bottom right)**, 253, 256–57:** Photographs. Andrew Bartlett, OOT Box Media

Page 250: Photographs, Kara Slating. Memorial Health

Page 252: Above left: Photograph by MK Pritzker

Page 254: Above: Mariah D. Smith Photography; bottom left and bottom right: photographs. Courtesy of the personal archives of Jesse White

Page 255: Above left, above right, and middle right: Mariah D. Smith Photography; bottom, courtesy of George Clinton & Parliament Funkadelic

Page 257: Above: Photograph by Christine Lovely; bottom: photograph by Marilyn Cagnoni

Page 260: Above: Illinois Secretary of State, "Photograph Files," DocHelm16900, Record Series 103.198, Illinois State Archives; bottom: DocHelm19055; back endpaper: DocHelm16769

Page 261: Photographs, above left: Abraham Lincoln Presidential Library and Museum; above right: *Illinois Centennial Bulletin*, Oct. 19, 1918, page 13; middle right: Matt Ferguson FergyPIX.com; bottom: Executive Mansion Collection; middle left: *Illinois State Register*, Jan. 1, 1940

MK (MARY KATHRYN) MUENSTER PRITZKER has served as Illinois's first lady since the inauguration of her husband, JB Pritzker, as governor in January 2019. In her work as first lady, MK builds on her lifelong commitment to advancing outcomes for women and girls in Illinois and beyond, with a focus on expanding access to reproductive health care and developing restorative criminal justice responsive to women's needs. The first lady also contributes her time to supporting LGBTQ+ initiatives and promoting the arts—most recently co-chairing the Arts for Illinois Relief Fund in response to the Covid-19 pandemic.

Having been educated in historic decorative arts and architecture, MK has used those skills to restore the Illinois Governor's Mansion to a welcoming home and public space that preserves the rich history and culture of the people of Illinois. Her work has brought to the mansion a carefully curated collection of fine art, crafts, and furniture. In addition, the first lady has meticulously researched and documented the mansion's cultural history and changing architecture over its almost 170-year life. She and acclaimed interior designer Michael S. Smith have worked together to create a home filled with warmth.

In addition to serving as first lady, MK is a member of the Committee for the Preservation of the White House. She previously served as a director of the Pritzker Family Foundation, which is primarily focused on women's health initiatives and early childhood development. Through the foundation, MK and her husband were engaged in the strategic plan for Northwestern Pritzker School of Law. Their donation will be used, in part, to pay for scholarships and grants to allow highly qualified students of all income levels to attend one of America's best law schools. The gift also supports the law school's social justice, entrepreneurship, and civil and human rights initiatives.

Born in Lincoln, Nebraska, and raised in South Dakota, MK previously worked on the staffs of former U.S. Senate Majority Leader Tom Daschle and former Governor and U.S. Senator Bob Kerrey. She graduated with a B.A. from the University of Nebraska–Lincoln and attended graduate school in the master of science in historic preservation program at the School of the Art Institute of Chicago. When not in Springfield, she resides in Chicago, Illinois, with JB, their daughter, Teddi, their son, Donny, and their dog, Lincoln.

ACKNOWLEDGMENTS

I would like to recognize my predecessors, the Illinois first ladies whose legacies have helped guide me on my own journey in public life. In this book I have tried to honor their contributions to community, state, and country. Without them, this glorious house, known as the People's House, would not have remained standing. I am especially grateful to Brenda Edgar, Jayne Carr Thompson, and Diana Rauner, who shared their experiences with me.

A chance meeting with Michael Smith on a very cold day in January 2009 during President Obama's inauguration turned into a cherished friendship, and since then he has become such a valuable supporter and compatriot in my public service. His immense talent spreads beauty and joy wherever he goes.

Margaret Russell has spent a lifetime documenting Americans and their interiors, and her contributions are embedded throughout this book. I'm grateful for everything she did to help me launch this book project and for her continual guidance.

I cannot imagine better partners than the Rizzoli team, whose excellent reputation is only exceeded by the quality of their people. Publisher Charles Miers took a chance on a first-time author, and I hope I have delivered on the promise. The secret sauce was my team of book pals: Sandy Gilbert Freidus, who provided skillful project editing and an eye for detail; Susan Sully, the master wordsmith, who spent considerable time in assisting me with my writing; and David Byars, who through his book layout design made everything more beautiful and perfect. His passion for historic preservation, shared by this group, is felt throughout these pages.

I thank my Illinois team wholeheartedly for making this book possible—beginning with my associate Christine Lovely, who was my support system at every turn through this and so many other facets of my life. Susan Benjamin gave me the confidence early on that I could do this and conducted research that was invaluable to the project. In Springfield, my chief of staff, Marilyn Cagnoni, has made my job as first lady better and more fun. And I'm indebted to the Governor's Mansion staff, Tammy Bradford, Chad Burrus, Malcolm Brown, Alicia Jordan-Johnson, Harry Lewis, and Thad Rebbe, who have managed to make this historic building a home for my family and me. To Team Scooby and the entire executive protection unit, who keep my family and me safe during our public service—a finer group of professionals does not exist.

The archivists, curators, historic preservationists, and museum professionals of Illinois who helped on this project truly represent the best of our state, especially historian Mark Johnson, who epitomizes excellence. His work is the basis for this book. My gratitude also goes to Chief of Acquisitions Ian Hunt and iconographer Megan Klintworth at the Abraham Lincoln Presidential Library and Museum for sharing their knowledge and giving me so much of their time, and to the staff and leadership of the Art Institute of Chicago and the Chicago History Museum for their research assistance.

The photographers Michael Mundy and Scott Shigley created the gorgeous photographs for this book that capture the beauty and warmth of the Governor's Mansion.

Oscar Shamamian, Stephen Chrisman, and Martin Burns of Ferguson & Shamamian Architects, I thank you for donating the beautiful hand-rendering of the 1855 mansion. This work of art will become part of the mansion's permanent collection to be enjoyed by visitors.

The Illinois Governor's Mansion Association is the steward of the People's House. I am grateful for its support during my tenure and the job it has done for the people of Illinois. Thank you to Leslie Hindman and to Joe Gromacki and his associates at Jenner & Block LLP. To John Forehand and Bulley & Andrews, who donate their time and expertise to the care of the mansion, I am so thankful for your guidance. Thank you to Craig Bergmann, the mansion's landscape designer, for keeping a keen eye on the garden and adding his lasting stamp to the grounds.

Finally, I would like to thank my husband, JB, who always gives his unwavering support to every project I embark upon. It would be impossible to imagine taking this journey of life without him, and it is made complete by our children, Teddi and Donny. To all three of them, my heart is full.

MICHAEL S. SMITH is considered one of the most original and respected talents in the design industry today. With an international roster of residential, hospitality, and commercial clients, Michael has a style that seamlessly blends European classicism and American modernism. A longtime member of the AD100 and *Elle Decor*'s A-List, he has authored numerous books, including *Designing History: The Extraordinary Art and Style of the Obama White House*—a celebration of his redecoration of the White House.

SUSAN S. BENJAMIN, through her firm Benjamin Historic Certifications, is an architectural historian with a career that spans over forty years. She is a celebrated author and speaker and one of Illinois's most knowledgeable architectural documentarians. Her publications include *Modern in the Middle: Chicago Houses 1929–1975* and *Great Houses of Chicago, 1871–1921*. Susan lives in Highland Park, Illinois, with her husband of fifty-five years, Wayne.

SUSAN SULLY is the author of many books about architecture and design, including *The Allure of Charleston: Houses, Rooms, and Gardens* and *Past Present: Living with Heirlooms and Antiques*. A graduate of Yale University with a degree in art history, Susan has contributed articles to *The New York Times*, *Town & Country Travel*, *Veranda*, and other publications.

Over the course of his more than thirty-year career, **MICHAEL MUNDY** has captured the essence of everything from architectural spaces and noted personalities to beauty and fashion products. Michael's photographs have been featured in many publications, among them *Architectural Digest*, *Town & Country*, *Martha Stewart Living*, and *The New York Times*. His commercial clients include some of the world's most renowned brands.

Chicago-based photographer **SCOTT SHIGLEY** has photographed the work of prominent landscape architects, as well as parks, public gardens, cultural institutions, and noted interiors. His photographs are regularly published in national and regional design publications. Scott brings his own original perspective to every project.

LEFT To commemorate Illinois's bicentennial in 2018, the Hinsdale Embroiderers' Guild, the second oldest embroiderers' guild in America, created a needlepoint portrait depicting the 1855 appearance of the mansion.

Design by David Byars

First published in the United States of America in 2023 by
Rizzoli International Publications, Inc.
300 Park Avenue South
New York, NY 10010
www.rizzoliusa.com

Publisher: Charles Miers
Editor: Sandra Gilbert Freidus
Editorial Assistance: Natalie Danford and Sara Pozefsky
Design Assistance: Olivia Russin
Production Manager: Maria Pia Gramaglia
Managing Editor: Lynn Scrabis

Printed in Italy

2023 2024 2025 2026 / 10 9 8 7 6 5 4 3 2 1

ISBN: 978-0-8478-7363-0
Library of Congress Control Number: 2023933601

Visit us online:
Facebook.com/RizzoliNewYork
instagram.com/rizzolibooks
twitter.com/Rizzoli_Books
pinterest.com/rizzolibooks
youtube.com/user/RizzoliNY
issuu.com/Rizzoli

FRONT COVER Portraits of President Abraham
Lincoln by Alban Jasper Conant and Michael
S. Nachtrieb hang in the Lincoln Parlor.

BACK COVER Morning light illuminates the
East Parlor, which is decorated with sunny
yellow-striped wallpaper and antique furniture
selected by Michael Smith and MK Pritzker.

ENDPAPERS Mauny wallpaper in the Empire
dessin Maïs pattern, inspired by a nineteenth-
century design, features a corn motif apt for
the Illinois theme of much of the mansion's
interior decoration. Zuber & Cie, distributed
by Brunschwig & Fils (SPREADS); A portrait
of Abraham Lincoln by Albert Meyer was
based on a photograph made by Chicago
photographer Alexander Hesler at Springfield
in June 1860, shortly after Lincoln became the
Republican candidate for president (FRONT);
Governor Dwight H. Green's daughter Gloria
is seen sledding down the driveway in 1943,
when the grounds of the mansion became a
wintertime play scene (BACK).